CULTURE AND THE PEOPLE

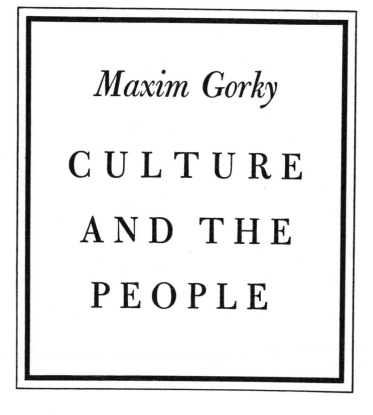

Maxim Gorky

CULTURE AND THE PEOPLE

BOOKS FOR LIBRARIES PRESS
FREEPORT, NEW YORK

STANDARD BOOK NUMBER:

8369-5373-8

LIBRARY OF CONGRESS CATALOG CARD NUMBER:

79-119930

PRINTED IN THE UNITED STATES OF AMERICA

PUBLISHER'S NOTE

THIS collection contains the last essays of Gorky which are related centrally to the theme stated in the title of this book—culture and the people. It is a representative selection from the voluminous publicist efforts in which the author was engaged during the last ten years of his life. Together with his bookful of articles, On Guard for the Soviet Union, *which we published in 1933, the present volume reveals a side of Gorky's writing as necessary to an understanding of his work as his novels, stories, autobiographical volumes and plays. Some of the contributions are slashing polemics; many were written under the pressure of daily journalism, appearing in numerous periodicals, including the leading Soviet papers* Pravda *and* Izvestia; *all of them reflect the vigor and depth of Gorky's literary talent.*

CONTENTS

vii

CULTURE AND THE PEOPLE

TEN YEARS

FOREIGNERS come from Europe to visit the Soviet Union. They spend two or three weeks among the Russians and then return home to recount what they have seen. They tell their story as though they were people with minds of such exceptional penetration that they require only twenty days or so to obtain a thorough understanding of the cultural progress that is taking place in a country with a population of a hundred and sixty million people, a country with whose past they are little acquainted and towards whose present they are emotionally inimical. As history has fostered in people the ability to do and perceive what is bad with greater zest and pleasure than what is good, it is only natural that our visitor friends should enjoy stressing the "mistakes" and "shortcomings" of the Soviet government, the "uncultured" state of the Russian people and their diabolical vices in general.

Another thing that influences judgments about Russia is a long-standing malady of Europeans, namely, the preposterously exaggerated and ludicrously inflated consciousness of their own superiority over the Russians. This malady is due to their profound ignorance of everything that concerns the Russian people. And, naturally, this remarkable capacity of the representatives of European culture to thoroughly misunderstand Russia in general, and modern Russia in particular, is enhanced by the fact that Messrs. Béraud, London and their ilk are obeying the will of those who send them, though I am prepared to grant that in doing so some of them do violence to their own personal wishes.

For all these reasons, investigators of Russian life, when relating their not overly malicious anecdotes, deliberately, or from ignorance or thoughtlessness, but above all, of course, as a result of their class psychology, tend to forget the difficult and complex conditions under which the Soviet government not only is performing its work of restoring the economic life that was shattered by the European War and the Civil War, but under which also a new culture is in process of being created. As to the active part taken by the "interventionist" powers in plundering and damaging Russia, these people are completely silent.

They are also silent about the fact that only six of these ten years have been devoted to creative work. The other four were taken up by the Civil War, which though it certainly served to impoverish the country still more, at the same time helped to sober the people, ridding them of sundry illusions and endowing them with a new psychology.

The Civil War would probably have continued to this day, if Vladimir Lenin and his comrades, at the risk of completely destroying the Party of Bolshevik workers by dissolving it in the mass of peasants, whom the war had turned into anarchists, had not pushed the Party into the most advanced posts and set it at the head of the peasantry. By doing this Lenin saved Russia from being utterly shattered and enslaved by the European capitalists—and history cannot but give him credit for it.

It is well known that the Russian bourgeoisie did its best to hand over the country to England and France; and to this very day it has not lost all hope of provoking a foreign invasion of Russia.

Ten Years

What was the heritage which the Bolshevik Party received when it took power into its own hands, and what were the conditions under which it has been working in the past six or seven years? Several millions of the healthiest and most able-bodied people of the country had perished in the war. A large section of the "revolutionary" intelligentsia went over to the side of the enemies of the people. Part of them went on strike, refusing to help the new régime in its fight for the liberation of the toiling masses, and thus the former opponents of the autocracy became "internal enemies" of their own people. The agriculture of the country, already in a state of collapse, continued to deteriorate under the attacks of the "White" armies. In the factories, which had always been badly equipped, the machinery had become thoroughly worn out during the war, and the Civil War had, in addition, destroyed a large number of the politically and culturally enlightened workers. In their place it had bequeathed to the Soviet régime the drastic legacy of a shattered system, calling into activity those degenerate types of people which are produced in large numbers by the capitalist system in all European countries. Such people would deliberately or automatically find their way into the Soviet organisation; and to this day, as we know, the government has been unable to rid itself entirely of them, as is proved by the recent trial of the Ryazan bandits. The governments of Europe have been doing their best to hamper the work of the Soviet government in the economic and cultural reorganisation of the country, while the Russian émigrés, supported by the European bourgeoisie, have been waging guerilla warfare on their own people, training spies and hired assassins and sending them into Russia. And to all this must be added the year of "famine."

Culture and the People

This is a brief, and of course incomplete, description of the conditions amidst which the Soviet government began and is continuing its work. One would have imagined that people who undertook to describe present-day Russia would not lose sight of such facts.

What, then, has the Soviet government achieved during these six years? In the first place, the Russian workers and peasants are learning to administer their own country. They are beginning to feel that the state is their own affair, and that liberty can be achieved only by the harmonious co-operation of all the forces in the country, united by the consciousness of the grandeur and difficulty of the tasks they have so courageously set out to accomplish. The working people of the world, slowly it is true, are coming more and more to realise the tremendous significance of this fact.

European intellectuals, the majority of whom are indifferent to the fate of their own people, would find much to envy were they better informed of what has been achieved in Russia. In the Soviet Union the work of the man of science, which is of such importance to human society, is appreciated at its full worth, as is testified by Russian scientists themselves, who during these ten years have been able to develop astonishingly fertile activities. They have their House of Scientists and their own rest home, institutions such as are not to be found in Europe. The Russian scientist is an active and influential collaborator of the government, as the respect with which many great scientists are treated bears witness. Their welfare and needs are as carefully considered as the still difficult economic conditions of the country permit. In Europe in the post-war period, the funds assigned for the maintenance and equipment of scientific institutions have been considerably curtailed; in

Russia, on the other hand, a number of institutes for research have been opened and several new universities founded; the study of the mineral wealth of the country has been placed on a broad footing and many new deposits of ores of various kinds have been discovered; a number of highly valuable scientific discoveries and technical inventions have been made; new methods of combating grain pests and other agricultural scourges are being applied; marshes are being drained, breeds of cattle improved, and so on. The electrification of the country is proceeding steadily, new factories are being built and new branches of production are gradually being developed.

A press of an absolutely unique kind has been created dealing with the interests of the workers and peasants down to the commonplace details and needs of their everyday life. Of almost equal cultural and political value with the big newspapers published in the various capitals, are the numerous small papers issued by the workers in their factories, printing-shops, and tramway depots—all the *Shuttles, Benches, Threshers, Tram Sparks,* in which the workers themselves are learning to write about their day-to-day problems and methods for increasing the productivity of labour, and in which the self-criticism of the workers eloquently testifies to their enhanced sense of dignity, their growing cultural demands, and their eager thirst for knowledge.

There is a whole army of *"rabcor"* (worker correspondents) and *"selcor"* (village correspondents), men and women who are playing an active part in the Soviet Union, besides great numbers of "women delegates," etc. This means that the people are being taught, and are rapidly learning, to speak freely about themselves, about their needs and desires. There is a growing army of Komsomols (Young Communist Leaguers) and they are followed by the Young Pioneers, children who are being taught to see things from the standpoint of the state as a whole.

The country districts are also catered to by newspapers, illustrated magazines, and pamphlets dealing with all phases of rural husbandry and published in hundreds of thousands of copies. And, in addition, there is the Radio Newspaper, which already has some five million listeners-in. The thirst for knowledge is spreading among the peasantry, and this is a sign of the growth of culture. Women are from year to year taking an increasing share in the political life of the country. Moslem women are being emancipated. Non-Russian nationalities are being brought into the general stream of cultural activity and are demanding their own capitals, which will lead to the growth of new cities. Kazan, for instance, is rapidly developing as the capital of the Tatar republic.

It may be said that the level of literacy among the peasantry nevertheless remains low. This is true. But schools are spreading. And, in addition, every year tens of thousands of educated Red Army men return to the villages, and thousands of working men come from the towns to spend their holidays in the villages. These make good teachers. We must also realise the tremendous cultural value of the electric lamp: during the long winter evenings it illuminates thousands of peasants' huts, its light attracting both literate and illiterate, who gather together to discuss what is happening in the world.

No one can accuse me of idealising the peasantry; but I assert that in the Soviet Union there is already a large number of peasants who are more widely and thoroughly acquainted with the life of the world, and more active culturally, than the peasants of any other country in Europe.

16

But the chief thing the European visitor will not and does not see is that in the Soviet Union vast numbers are being drawn into public life, that the people are rapidly discarding the psychology induced in them by centuries of slavery, that they are beginning to conceive the state as an organisation of people pursuing a common aim, and not as an anarchic and mechanical conglomeration of individuals, divided into hostile classes and castes.

This, I shall be told, is a mere panegyric. And, indeed, it is a panegyric! For all my life my only heroes have been those who enjoy work and are able to work, those whose aim it is to liberate all the forces of humanity for creative work, in order to make our world more beautiful and to organise forms of life on earth that are worthy of mankind.

To this end the Bolsheviks are striving with astonishing energy, and with a success that is evident to all honest people who do not allow themselves to be blinded by rancour. All over the world the working people are beginning to understand the significance of this work and to realise the part they themselves must play.

Ten years have passed, yet the Soviet system still exists and is growing steadily stronger, is causing profound vexation to certain would-be Masaryks by its virility.

In the Soviet Union the foundation of a new world is really being laid. Such a foundation I take to be the liberation of the once fettered will to live; that is to say, the will to act, for life is action. The free labour of men has everywhere been desecrated and violated by senseless and cynical exploitation. The capitalist system has destroyed the pleasure of creating things; it has turned labour from a free expression of man's creative force into a curse. This everybody knows.

17

Culture and the People

But in the Soviet Union people are beginning to work in the knowledge that their labour is of value to the state, in the knowledge that through labour lies the shortest and most direct road to freedom and culture. The Russian worker does not earn a mere pittance, as in the old days—he is earning a state of his own. He feels that he is gradually becoming the master of his country and the leader of the peasantry on its way to freedom. He is learning, too, that the whole world belongs to the working man; that science gives him this world as raw material for the creation of use values and is mastering the forces of nature in order to lighten the burden of human toil. Soon he will come to understand that labour creates not only material values but something far greater, namely, the confidence of man in the power of reason, and the conviction that it is his mission to overcome by his rational will all obstacles that stand in its way.

The Russian worker remembers what was urged by his leader, Vladimir Lenin, and is rapidly learning to govern his state—this is a fact whose significance cannot be exaggerated.

One of the great merits of the Soviet government is that it has created a press which is broadly and skilfully acquainting the population of the Union with the life of the outside world and is ruthlessly exposing the falsity and vileness of this life.

The Russian people are being constantly influenced by the free and stern truth about everything that is going on in the world: the shameless brutality and unbridled will of the ruling classes, how they are degenerating and losing their reason, and how the healthy will to live of the enslaved is growing to replace them. This is the most important thing to know, and the Soviet press is making it known.

When one has lived some three-score years, one gets rather tired of man's "bad" qualities, and begins to experience the

18

need to observe some of his "good" qualities. This need is not a result of fatigue; not at all. It arises from the consciousness of how much effort the modern Russian must make in order to overcome the "old Adam" within him—the legacy of centuries. It is a known and incontestable fact that nowhere is the capitalist system capable of producing a "good" man. And when one recalls the conditions in which the Russian of thirty-five or forty-five years of age, who is now engaged in building a new life, was brought up, one is astonished not so much that he has retained some of his bad qualities, but that he is no worse than he is, and is, moreover, steadily improving. I am not inclined to underrate what is bad in him, but neither am I inclined to demand of a man what he is as yet unable to give.

I have known the builder of modern Russian life ever since his youth. At first he was a "whipped boy," the stepson of the horrible Russian life; he then passed through underground revolutionary activity to prison, exile, and penal servitude; and then he made the great revolution that really did "shake the world," and will continue to shake it until it collapses. Then for three years he waged a civil war that ended victoriously; and having ended it, he set about the difficult job of restoring the shattered economic life of Russia, a job for which he had no more training than for the job of beating highly-trained generals on the Civil War fronts. Now he is working as an administrator twelve and fourteen hours a day; his living conditions are poor, not much better than those of a manual labourer, but he is performing a job which, apart from its historical significance, is distinguished by extreme complexity.

He has never had the opportunity of cultivating the qualities which were, and still are, the boast of the Russian intellectuals, who made so little ado about scurrying into the camp of his enemies, thereby showing that their "qualities"—socialism and humanism, for instance—were merely a matter of words.

He is no phrasemonger, he is no "god-seeker," but a splendid, honest worker of this world, who has definitely rejected the ancient lies and has boldly gone his own road towards freedom—the only road that leads to it directly.

There was a time, during the gloomy years of reaction, 1907-10, when I called him a "god-builder," meaning by this that both within himself and on earth man creates and embodies the capacity to perform miracles of justice and beauty, and all the other miracles which idealists attribute to a power that supposedly exists outside of man. Man's labour tends to convince him that, except for his reason and will, there is no miraculous power apart from the forces of nature, and that these he must master so that they may serve his reason and will, and thus lighten his labour and life. He believes that "only man exists—all else is thought and deed."

This man is a man the like of whom the world has never seen. And this man has set himself the tremendous task of shaping the mass of the toiling people "in his own form and image"—a task which he is performing with no little success. At all events, he is an incontestable proof of the abundant creative force and talents that lie concealed in the mass of the working folk.

He is fully worthy, one would think, of the admiration and respect of all who are disgusted with the monstrous and cynical chaos of life; and he is particularly worthy of the respect of the former *narodolyubtsi,* the "people-lovers," who used with such readiness and gusto to bewail the sufferings of their "little brother."

Yet these former "people-lovers" have made this builder of

a new life a target for all their mud-slinging and slander. The ammunition for this sterile pastime is supplied by the press of the Soviet Union, which mercilessly depicts and pillories the diseases of the old order with which its people are still infected. The newspapers of the Soviet Union daily print a great deal of material that draws attention to disgusting aspects in social life. That is an honourable and necessary job. But this material provides the most tasty morsels for those people who are themselves already of no use in life. The émigré journalists and columnists smack their lips in malicious glee over this "swinishness," chew it over with maniacal delight, and then belch it forth again. Nature and habit are, of course, at work here. They are the sort of people who get no pleasure out of life unless they see only its filthy side; only then are they conscious of their own purity and innocence. During the period of reaction they were fond of quoting, "the darker the night, the brighter the stars"; and when they said stars, they meant themselves. But they are simply people whom history has discarded, and who are condemned to lead a bitter existence, tormented by impotent rage. They shout and splutter because there is nothing else they can do. But history has already hurled at them an imperious: "Silence!"

It is not for me to describe what can better be described by others—the great projects that have been completed in Russia during the past ten years.

My joy and my pride is the new Russian man, the builder of the new state.

To this small, but great man, who is to be found in all the remotest and wildest parts of the country, in factories and villages, and cast away in the steppe and the Siberian taiga, in the Caucasian mountains and in the Northern tundra; to the man who is sometimes very lonely, working among people who still find it hard to understand him; to the servant of his state, who is modestly performing a job that seems to be insignificant, but whose historical significance is tremendous—to him I address my sincere greetings.

Comrade, be steadfast in the knowledge that you are the most necessary man on earth! In doing your small job, you have really begun to create a new world.

Learn and teach others!

I warmly shake your hand, comrade!

1927

TO THE ANONYMOUS
AND PSEUDONYMOUS

THE newspaper *Ruhl* has reprinted from the newspaper *Dni* *
a "Reply to Gorky," which is evidently an answer to my article
on the tenth anniversary of the October Revolution. The author of the "Reply" puts the following question to me:

"What induces you to flatter our villains so servilely and to
say nothing about their crimes? Your words (about the knowledge of the value of labour to the state under the Soviet régime)
burn into our brain; for while we march with red flags in our
hands, to 'demonstrate' our enthusiasm, our wives and mothers
stand in queues for milk, flour, and butter."

Then follows abuse.

I have to inform the author of the "Reply" and his confrères
that I have been receiving wretched little letters like his for a
long time, and that I receive them quite often. At first it was
members of the "Black Hundreds" who used to write me just
such savage letters, threatening me with all sorts of dire things
just as ridiculous as those I am now threatened with by people
who fifteen to twenty years ago were, I thought, sincere
enemies of everything pertaining to the Black Hundreds and
reaction. Literature of this sort did not prevent me from doing
my job then, it does not prevent me from doing it now, and
will not prevent me from doing it in the future. As an old

* Russian counter-revolutionary papers published abroad.—*Trans.*

23

bird-catcher, I can tell a bird by its note without seeing it. And I also know that "reforms" like that of Peter I, for example, were always disparaged by people who had found life sweet under the old order.

But it is not Peter the Great who is active in the Soviet Union to-day; it is Ivan the Great—the worker and peasant under one cloak; and it is not a matter of "reforms," but of a radical alteration of the whole foundation of the old life. It is therefore only natural that lovers of the comfortable past should hurl vilification and abuse at the workers' and peasants' government which is indefatigably leading the whole mass of the toiling people to a new life.

I know that in Russia there was, and still is, much that is bad; I have reason to believe that I know this better than the authors of the anonymous letters. But never has the good been so good as it is in Russia now. And nowhere has the bad been so pitilessly exposed, nowhere has it been so strenuously fought as in Soviet Russia.

The authors of the anonymous letters, like Mr. Dan * of the *Sotsialistichesky Vestnik*, want to know why I do not say now what I said in 1917. My reply is that in 1917 I was mistaken, sincerely fearing that the dictatorship of the proletariat would lead to the dispersion and destruction of the politically trained Bolshevik workers, the only real revolutionary force, and that their destruction would result in the very idea of a social revolution being eclipsed for a long time to come. At that time a large number of intellectuals also realised that they had been mistaken in believing themselves a revolutionary force. Ten years have since elapsed, and in this interval an astonishing amount of work has been accomplished in Russia in all spheres

* Russian émigré, Menshevik leader.—*Trans.*

of labour and creative effort, although this work has been hindered, and is still being hindered, in every way by "cultured" Europe, whose bourgeoisie is zealously encouraged by the Russian émigrés, people who were "mistaken," and who are disgustingly incensed with their mistakes, as well as with the consciousness of their own insignificance. I do not flatter the workers' and peasants' régime; I sincerely admire its work and its ability to inspire people to work and creative activity. You are not pleased that I admire it? It would be strange if you were. I must say that I do not ever recall wanting to "please" anybody, let alone people of your type of mind. Of course, I do not protest against the vile abuse and threats, the lies and calumnies which you so zealously bestow upon me just because you have "nothing else to do." I know that freedom of abuse is your motto and your pastime. And what would you do if you were unable to lie?

Mr. Dan said that before having my greetings to the workers' and peasants' government published in an English newspaper, I "deemed it proper to submit it to the authorities for approval." Nobody with the least "decency" or "self-respect" would have written anything so vulgar; Mr. Dan did.

Then, in strange unison¹ with the anonymous, he cries out against the "brutality" of the workers' and peasants' government, evidently forgetting the recent past, the wholesale shootings of workers, the "Lena affair," the Jewish pogroms of 1903, January 9, 1905, and much else of the same kind, the Amur cart road, the tens of thousands sent into exile, the abominable war of 1914-18, and, finally, what the White generals did in Russia with the gracious assistance of certain Russian "revolutionaries" and a host of "higher" intellectuals. Apparently, Mr. Dan does not understand the brutality that arises in the people in revenge for the innumerable and cynical torments they have suffered, nor the bitterness of self-defence of a people that is surrounded by known and secret traitors and irreconcilable enemies. This bitterness has been provoked, and it is therefore justified.

But there is also the bitterness of parasites who are accustomed to live at the expense of the enslaved, and who are trying once more to enslave a people that has won its liberty. This bitterness cannot be justified.

I remind Mr. Dan of this not by way of controversy, of course, but for his edification.

1927

THE RED ARMY

ONE great and indisputable achievement of the Soviet government is the formation of the Red Army. It would be interesting to estimate the number of educated men which the Red Army, during the years of its existence, has conferred upon the countryside. How many of its men have qualified as chairmen of rural district and village executive committees of the Soviets? How many men have left the Red Army to enter universities or to attend university preparatory courses? How many of them are working on the staffs of Red Army newspapers? How many have become highly skilled workers? And generally, what is the number of cultured people who have been educated by an army which, in all the tragic history of Europe, is the first and only real people's army, formed not for attack but for defence?

When I inspected the magnificent House of the Red Army in Moscow, when I attended courses in the first elements of education given to men in the camps and saw the way they were being trained in the field, my mind conjured up the gloomy picture of recruitment levies in the old days, the barrack life of the tsarist soldiers, the coarseness and brutality of their training, and all the savage horror that attended the manufacture of "cannon fodder." The Red Army has left this past far behind; never will our fighters allow anybody to turn them back to this past, for every such turn would mean directing their struggle against themselves, instead of for themselves and for the preservation of what their fathers and elder broth-

27

ers have won. It also occurred to me that while I was freely conversing with the Red Army men, the camps and barracks of Europe were filled with peasants and workers who were being zealously trained for the shameful business of mutual extermination, for a new carnage which would be even more horrible than the carnage of 1914-18; and which would inflict upon the world millions of corpses, tens of thousands of cripples, thousands driven insane by terror, millions of widows and orphans. Once again towns and villages would be destroyed, fields trampled, fertile land laid waste, and every effort made to wipe out the magnificent fruits of man's labour, to destroy culture.

It occurred to me that tens and hundreds of thousands of workers in the factories of Europe were engaged in manufacturing guns, rifles, explosives, and poison gas—all for the purpose of murdering each other. Why, for whose sake was the extermination of working people by working people required? For the sake of the score or so thousand of very wealthy and utterly irresponsible people who "rule the world," that is, who live on the labour of others, on the blood of others, and who infect the working people with the diseases of greed, envy, and enmity, as lice infect with typhus.

To this handful of morally obtuse and degenerate people who, relying on the blindness and lack of will of the working masses, rule the world, the Soviet government has proposed two plans of disarmament. The first plan envisaged complete disarmament and the closing down of all factories that manufacture the wherewithal for the wholesale murder of people—murder which, for some reason or other, is not considered a crime. If this proposal had been accepted by the governments of Europe, it would have released huge sums of gold that are now being expended for the extermination of working people, who are being armed to attack one another. Hundreds of billions might have been used for lightening the burden of labour, for creating easier conditions of life, for advancing culture, and for furthering agriculture. Of course, the people who command the disgusting realities of life, the people who have created this onerous and shameful mode of living that is full of irreconcilable contradictions, antagonisms, enmity, and crime, refused to disarm.

They also refused the second proposal, which was to disarm not fully, but partially. This refusal was tantamount to an admission that they cannot exist without wars, without a wholesale murder. This refusal was tantamount to an admission that their power is founded on hundreds and thousands of armed workers and peasants, whose physical strength is the sole source of the power and wealth of the bourgeoisie. They rob the working people and compel the people they rob to defend them. That is the simple foundation of the rule of the bourgeoisie. It must be said that those who allow themselves to be robbed, and at the same time defend the robbers with arms in hand, are also . . . simpletons. In general, it is all astonishingly simple, and quite comprehensible, except for one thing: how is it that the working people are so slow in understanding the vileness of this simplicity?

Imagine the following scene: a common murderer has been caught, caught by kind-hearted people, who say to him:

"Throw away your knife. Stop killing people. It is wrong."

"I can't," he answers. "If I stop killing I shall have nothing to live on."

This simple answer is the answer the European governments gave to the proposal made on behalf of the Soviet government

Culture and the People

by M. M. Litvinov. And having given this simple and clear answer, the bourgeoisie of Europe continues to whet its knife against the workers' and peasants' régime in the Soviet Union. The building of a new life in the Soviet Union is progressing under difficult conditions: but it is progressing successfully, and the achievements in various fields of labour are astonishing, if the complexity of the conditions in which our working people are living and labouring is not lost sight of. There can be no doubt that the achievements would have been even greater if the people had not been obliged to expend huge resources on their self-defence, on their army. The enemy is voracious, cunning, and rich; there is enough "cannon fodder" to be bought, and he is in a position to buy it. He can buy Rumanians, Poles and—but are there not enough purblind people in the world who have not yet grown wise enough to understand their own true interests! Our working people should know this; but they can face the future without fear. They have a splendid defensive force, not only because it has good bayonets, but chiefly because it has been armed with an invincible truth, it has been taught to understand the inhumanity of the "simplicity" of the capitalist state. The Red Army is not only a fighting force; it is also a cultural force. It is a powerful organisation that draws vast masses of the working population of the Soviet Union into public and state cultural work. It gives excellent assistance to the spread of the cultural revolution by introducing literacy to the rural districts; and the cultural revolution is the only force that can help the Soviet Union to outstrip the capitalist countries in the development of its productive forces and in its speed of economic growth. In preparing to defend the country, the Red Army has already assumed the offensive against the economic and political inertia of the masses, and against their ancient prejudices and ingrained misconceptions.

That this is so, is very eloquently borne out by the attitude of the young peasants towards service in the army. Such an attitude towards the army as is displayed in the Soviet Union, where the young men regard it as a cultural and educational institution, is scarcely possible anywhere else in the world. I know of a number of instances when groups of peasant youths of recruiting age, over and above the fixed contingent, persistently requested to be enrolled under the colours. That was last October. No one will venture to say that such a thing ever occurred in the old days, when the recruits would march to the barracks singing:

> *Oh, it's hell to be living in barracks;*
> *This is the end of us!*

In the Soviet Union the Red Army man is trained to be a builder of a new culture. He is not only the defender of his people; in many respects, and to a growing extent, he is becoming its teacher.

People who have been deprived of the possibility of living at the expense of others, cry and groan, Russia is perishing! But it is they who are perishing, and terror at their inevitable doom inspires them with the belief that together with them are perishing the one hundred and sixty millions of a talented people, which, nevertheless, is successfully building a state for itself almost with its bare hands.

Many disgusting survivals of the accursed, vile, and disgraceful past still remain in this great and splendid country of "unlimited possibilities." But it has already achieved the main thing: its working folk have come to feel profoundly the invincibility of the force of knowledge, and, having come to feel it, they are learning to work well and to live in a new way. The schools, universities, and workers' university preparatory courses are filled to overflowing with healthy and intelligent young people; their striving for education is so great that, although seventy thousand young people are obliged to content themselves with the lectures of the "Home University," tens of thousands of applicants cannot find a place in the higher educational establishments. That is bad, but, like everything that is bad, it is temporary. The Red Army is also a school that provides a cultural training for young people. And the men of the Red Army fully understand that they are not only defenders of their country against the foreign enemy, but that they must also be fighters against the enemy at home—the old stupidities, wretched habits, and superstitions—fighters on behalf of the new culture.

1928

ON THE LITERATURE
OF THE WHITE ÉMIGRÉS

FOR six years I have read the émigré press. At first I read and asked myself in perplexity—in naïve perplexity:

Is it possible that these variously stupid publicists are the same Russian intellectuals who used to teach themselves and the "lesser brother" the feeling of "holy hatred" for the life which was poisoned from top to bottom with hypocrisy, malice, and falsehood? Was it they who admired the works of such iconoclasts as the sullen Swift, the mercilessly taunting Voltaire, or the stupendously great Tolstoy? Was it they who taught their children to love the marvellously conceived figure of the holy knight of La Mancha?

The heroes of their youth were Spartacus, Fra Dolchino, Wat Tyler, Thomas Muenzer, Jan Huss, and all those men and women who, out of their flesh and blood, wanted to create liberty, something that had never lived on earth but was absolutely necessary for mankind.

The favourite songs of their youth were the songs of robbers, romantic songs of protest, ballads about Razin, the angry poems of Nekrassov. It seemed that their true religion was "social romanticism."

To-day all this no longer raises any echo, their souls have gone numb. Apparently the Bolshevik "materialists" are right when they say that, confronted with grim reality, ideology easily yields to the most vicious zoological class psychology.

In no other country were the conditions of life subjected to such sharp and exhaustive criticism as among the intelligentsia in Russia. Nowhere was so much praise lavished on saints and sinful iconoclasts—Christ, Byron, Nietzsche, and all those who brought into life "not peace, but a sword." The Russian intelligentsia considered and called itself the "most advanced intelligentsia of Europe," it was eminently revolutionary in sentiment.

It is hard to understand where and to what purpose all this force was spent so soon: all the painstakingly accumulated knowledge about the suffering of the people and its attempts to throw off the yoke of tyranny, all the stored-up hatred for a life that distorted the whole nation, all the thirst for justice and "love for the people," a love which the intellectuals vowed to one another orally and in print, loudly, publicly, and immodestly.

I never vowed "love for the people"; I merely knew and know to-day that it is necessary to create the conditions for the Russian peasant in which he will quickly learn to live and work more rationally, conditions which will give him the opportunity to develop all his talents. But I sincerely believed that there were people who really "loved" the people, who possessed a special supernatural sense of which I happened to be deprived. One day I shall tell the story of how the revolutionary intelligentsia destroyed this belief in me. But, still, it was very distressing and painful to me to observe, in 1917, when the frenzied people, moving like a grey avalanche, left the front and bent its course towards the villages, raising over the land its broad and at last angry "mug,"—it was painful to see how, by its realism and anarchism, this "mug" at once scared off the "love" of the intelligentsia, the nightingale of its soul. The nightingale flew away into the brushwood of oblivion, and the black raven of philistine wisdom was enthroned in its place.

And immediately it became clear that all the vigour of a critical attitude towards life, all the force of ruthless, genuine, and active revolutionism, turned out to be in the possession of the "Bolsheviks."

I have not forgotten what my position was in those days. I remember that when V. A. Bazarov, also a Bolshevik, publicly, in the press, called his comrades "bunglers," I did not feel particularly offended on their behalf, although there were among them people whom I sincerely loved and respected. I was sure that the "people" would sweep away the Bolsheviks together with all the other socialist intellectuals and, what is most important, together with the organised workers. Then the only force capable of saving the country from anarchy, and of Europeanizing Russia, would have perished. But, thanks to the superhuman energy of Vladimir Lenin and his comrades, this did not happen.

What did happen was that almost all the "revolutionary" intelligentsia refused to take part in the work of the Revolution; they refused to do even cultural work, which is all the more necessary in times of storm than in times of "peace"—if such times ever exist on earth. And in so far as cultural work did go on at all, it was almost always—as I know it all too well— hostile to the people who had assumed power. I often realised that this was hostility by force of habit, traditional hostility, because these people knew how to "be hostile" in words, and had never learned anything else.

Of course, I know that, in spite of everything, there were quite a number of intellectuals who did not quit their places, but continued to work under conditions of hunger, cold, hostile suspicion, and senseless mockery at the hands of the police sergeants and gendarmes of the new power, at the hand of the "lesser brother" whose hostile attitude to the intelligentsia was the work not only of Akimov-Makhnovetz,* but also, as you know, of far bigger people.

The intellectuals who have stayed on in Russia continue their heroic work to this day. It is not they who write letters for the émigré newspapers "from Russia," "from Moscow," "from the provinces," letters that are obviously clumsily fabricated somewhere outside of Russia. I know personally that, in some cases, the words "from Moscow" should read "from the suburbs of Berlin."

The naïve perplexity which I experienced when reading the émigré press turned to disgust during the period of Lenin's illness.

Having lived on this earth for more than half a century, I have seen many stupidities and read of many more. But I cannot recall anything like the loathsome baiting, the mad grunting, the stream of lies and calumnies which were poured out by the "cultured" émigrés on the occasion of the illness and death of the man who over-exerted himself working for the regeneration of Russia, of the country which had been brought to ruin by the most stupid autocracy, by the most shameful of wars, and by the savage hooliganism of ignorant generals who had been "saving Russia" by destroying cities and killing off the people they professed "to love."

There is nothing that can compare with the shamelessness, cynicism, and falsity of the émigré press, except perhaps its hypocrisy. I am no admirer of the literary methods of those

* Russian Social-Democrat.—*Trans.*

White Émigré Literature

publicists who cannot differentiate between freedom of opinion and unrestrained license of expression, and if in this article I also express myself sharply, the reason for it is, not that I have any desire to imitate the hooligans of the émigré press, but only that I cannot find more precise words in which to compress all my contempt and disgust.

There is no greater impudence than to speak of the "bloodthirstiness" of the Bolsheviks, while those who organised the world carnage of the nations that lasted for four years are still alive, and while all those gentlemen who to-day so zealously strangle and kill people in the name of "the peace of the whole world" are still alive.

There is no greater hypocrisy than to cry out about the cruelty of the Reds while passing over in silence the sadistic punishment meted out to the Reds, of which the Whites so shamelessly boast in their memoirs. Why not reprint in their newspapers the following story, for example, told by Denisov, in *Svobodniye Mysli* (*Free Thoughts*):

> The liberator of Kuban, General Pokrovsky, who ordered two thousand prisoners to be hacked to pieces in Maikop (autumn of 1918) and who has since made it a rule not to take prisoners alive, has deep-set black eyes—the soft, intent, radiant eyes of a child or a languid woman.
>
> "Well, what else shall we entertain you with?" he said with a lazy movement of his hands. "Perhaps you'd like to look over my album of views of Kamishin...."
>
> He held out an album in a pink velvet binding with leather corners, rather large and bulky. On the first page there was a photograph: A small house with the St. George's flag of the commander waving from the roof and,

in front, the general sitting with his adjutants, regarding four men who had been hanged. . . .

On the next page: Two men hanging by their necks, on the high bank of the Volga, both wearing the insignia of Red officers on their sleeves. . . . The third page: A city square, with civilians hanging.

An adjutant explained: "We captured several people with political convictions. We reported to the general and asked what to do, as we'd got some prisoners. So he says: 'Blockheads! the people with ideals are exactly the ones who ought to be hanged. If you get one without ideals you can give him a flogging and some vodka, and send him off to fight. But what can you do with people who have ideals'? . . ."

The fourth page: Just a tree, and something swinging from it. . . . "Nature requires human nature," the general smiled with his eyes only. "Like Poussin I have no use for inanimate nature. . . ."

We all laughed and proceeded to the next car for supper. After the champagne two young Armenians (with a balalaika and a mandolin) played gipsy romances and folk songs for a long time.

There are many such stories, and I recommend them to Mr. Melgunov's * attention; he could make another book of them.

It is strange how easily these people have forgotten such memorable and instructive acts of cruelty as January 9, 1905, in St. Petersburg, January 13 in Riga, the extermination of Letts by General Beckmann and the Ostsee barons, the vengeance

---

* Historian, member of the Russian Constitutional Democratic Party (Cadets).—*Trans.*

wreaked by Generals Rennenkampf and Meller-Zakomelsky on the people in Siberia, the punishment meted out to the Georgians, and all the other bloody feats of the "pacifiers" in the years 1906-07; the Jewish pogroms, the mass murder of workers on the Lena, in Zlatoust and everywhere else, the Orel and other penal prisons, the Amur cart road, and the innumerable other bloody lessons which the autocracy taught the Russian people—a people inclined to cruelty, I maintain, even if it had not undergone these experiences. To console the admirers of the people, I will say that even in his cruelty, the Russian is exceptionally talented. I cannot deny even to you, gentlemen, this particular talent although, so far, your cruelty has found expression only in words. But I think that, if only . . . you would massacre a lot of people!

It goes without saying that I have no desire to justify anybody's cruelty. But, after all, we must admit the indisputable fact that not a single nation of Europe has gone through such a terrible university of blood, torture, and cynical mass murder as the Russian people; not one of them has been given such abject and harmful instruction along these lines as the Russian people. It is well known that beginning with 1905 the Russian sailors have suffered incredible tortures. It is well known how unbearably hard was the life of the Russian soldiers; and how mercilessly and with what sadistic pleasure they used to flog the Russian peasants. The Russian people have become so unpleasantly red for you because it had been soaked from head to foot in its own blood.

There are some who try to assure me that all this brutality has left no trace, and that the people preserved within themselves what is supposed to be a kind, gentle, specifically Russian soul, which neither feels nor remembers pain or insults, bears no ill-will and forgives everything.

But Ossorgin is right: such a soul would really have been dead! Fortunately for the splendid Russia of the future, she no longer has a soul like this, even if we grant that once it did exist. Her soul has awakened from its stupor, it is angry and, gradually manifesting its will to live, it is growing wiser and stronger.

It is in no gentle and magnanimous way that it manifests its will to live; it is, on the contrary, awe-inspiring. After all, it is not as yet a healthy soul, it still remembers all too well the recent, terrible past and is afraid of its return. It is poisoned with the venom of vengeance. And you must admit that it has a right to hate, that it has plenty to avenge. The fact of the matter is that the Russian Revolution was much less bloody than might have been expected. It would have been even less bloody, if you, gentlemen, had behaved with decency, more in keeping with your gifts and abilities; if you had not become involved in the intrigues of generals, and had not invited intervention. The Revolution would have developed more peacefully and successfully, if you had been able to forget the mistakes of those who acted boldly, the "inconveniences" which you experienced, and the injuries you personally suffered. But because of your egotism you are unable either to forget or to understand. At bottom you are just as stupidly vindictive as the ignorant Russian peasantry, whether clad in the peasant's rags or the soldier's greatcoat, or the sailor's uniform. In words, at least, you are the same brutes, but of course, far more contemptible.

I was told that after the murder of Uritsky,* a sailor who,

* Bolshevik leader, assassinated by Socialist-Revolutionists in 1918.—*Trans.*

in executing some people that perhaps were innocent of any guilt, hurled the command:

"Platoon—at the scoundrels—fire!"

Whereupon he went mad.

My dear sirs! I am no sadist; and when I am compelled to speak to you the way I do, I experience no pleasure at causing people pain, the kind of pleasure which you feel in every word you write in your newspapers against Russia and the Bolsheviks.

It seems to me that you too, all of you, have gone mad; but not because of a feeling of horror at carrying out executions prompted by revenge, like that unfortunate sailor. No, you have gone mad because of your malice, the petty malice of ambitious people who have forever lost their place in life.

You are as conceited as you are ungifted, as over-weening as you are impotent. Your impotence is an historical, an incontestable, fact; and neither the Whiteguard generals nor the "Interventionists" could aid that impotence. We have only to remember how easily the generals made you serve their ends, their crude, their openly thieving ends.

Ever since then, the primary feeling by which you have been guided, has been simply the sense of personal injury. True, a certain allowance should be made for this feeling. You did play a considerable part in the development of Russian culture, you were quite energetic workers in that sphere. But this work does not justify your conceit, and it cannot justify your savage hatred for the people who were not afraid to take power into their hands and who, to-day, govern Russia. And they do govern—however hard you may try not to see the successes of the Soviet government and not to believe in them.

Yes, they govern ruthlessly in Russia; but remember that it

is the country where every police sergeant used to feel that he was Ivan the Terrible, and every intellectual thought that he was deciding the destinies of the world. Constantin Leontyev and Nechayev were related in spirit, and so were Dostoyevsky and Pobedonostsev,* and they were very Russian men.

You who invoked the "twelve tongues" against the Russian people should be the last to talk about cruelty. Particularly now, when malice has driven you wild, as can be seen by your shameful attitude to the work and death of Lenin—the man whose name will forever remain the pride of Russia and the whole world, the man of whom the outstanding idealist of our time, Romain Rolland, said: "Lenin is the greatest man of our age, and the most unselfish."

Lenin will remain for all time a part of the history of Russia, while you, wasted by idleness, malice, and spleen, will soon go down into your graves. And, indeed, it is time you did, in order to avoid the possibility of once again changing your front and your landmarks. For, although to-day you are engaged in hostilities against the Bolsheviks, who can tell whose lackey to-day's "respectable" Russian will be to-morrow? You know yourselves how easily and simply people of your kidney go over to the camp of their enemies. And you are probably not mistaken when you suspect many of your friends of having ulterior, self-seeking motives for becoming renegades.

Soon you will quit this world, in which your rotten malice is of use to nobody but yourselves—and, for all I know, even you yourselves are probably, by this time, sick of your own malice. But the Bolsheviks will remain. Retreating and again advancing to their aim, working in an atmosphere of misconception and slander, of lying and beastly howls and grunts, they march

* Procurator of Holy Synod in tsarist Russia, reactionary.—*Trans.*

forward, raising the Russian peasantry to follow them. Your children will desert you and join the Bolsheviks. Without noticing it yourselves, you are teaching your children to understand your impotence and are gradually instilling in them contempt for their fathers as moral bankrupts.

But—supposing that the Bolsheviks had gone, and the road was free for you to return to Russia. Ask yourselves, with the remnants of your conscience: What could you bring the Russian people to-day? The fact is you have nothing left and, moreover, you would no longer find the "people," whom, in any case, you never knew well and of whom, to-day, you have no idea at all. Personally I am certain that in Russia you would only increase the number—the remnants—of the poor in spirit and of the perversely malicious.

All your talk about your love for Russia, about humanism and other things of the same order is absolutely idle. From force of habit, mechanically, you still think of yourselves as humanists, and so you still remember that Jew-baiting, for example, is a nasty thing; but of Letts and, in general, of "aliens" you speak the language of an anti-Semite about Jews. How can one believe in your humanism, when one reads your writings and feels with what sadistic pleasure you note every mistake and failure in Russia and how sincerely you are grieved by any success?

No matter what you may say of the Bolsheviks, they have taken upon themselves a burden of stupendous weight, they have set themselves a task that is superhuman, because this task means the realisation of everything that the wisest and most sincerely humane people of the world have dreamed of.

There is no room for you among these people. For you the game is up. It was a cruel and bloody game. I repeat: it is idle for you to talk about humanism. Your malice merely exposes the shameful ugliness of your intolerance.

Nobody in Europe bewailed life so loudly as the Russian intelligentsia. The whole of the intelligentsia was chained to the shackles of the capitalist state, this lifeless and corrupted state which was poisoning the people. The teachers of the intelligentsia, Gogol, Dostoyevsky, Tolstoy, rightly maintained that life was loathsome because of its deception and hypocrisy, because of its beastliness, its cynical egotism.

And because of its naked cynicism, life is becoming ever more loathsome. One can hardly breathe in the atmosphere of hatred, malice, vindictiveness. The clouds, growing ever thicker, threaten to break in the last storm, a storm which will destroy and sweep away all the cultural achievements of humanity; and only Russia works against this possibility. The Union of Socialist Soviets is ideologically organizing the working people of the whole world.

We cannot disentangle ourselves from the clutching cobweb of the ugly relationships of classes, parties, and groups, except by sweeping away the whole cobweb at once.

It is precisely in Russia that the most essential "work of our age" has been started, and the attempt to shift life from the three pillars of stupidity, envy, and greed—on to the bases of reason, justice, and beauty is being accomplished. This work awakes the sincere attention and sympathy of all honest people throughout the world, it stirs the thought of millions of human beings. In you, the "ex-heroes," this work manifestly excites only malice. I say manifestly, because I am certain that, in secret, you cannot help being envious of the Bolsheviks. For, here are people who live, work, and will live, and who are absolutely confident that no other power but theirs is possible in Russia.

They are complete strangers to the psychology of prisoners and are free of any fetishist attitude to the chains and shackles of the state idea. They boldly ignore the "destinies of history," although in word they do, it seems, recognise its laws. But actually they do things bluntly, *muzhik*-like, confident that:

Fate is no judge for us, we are the masters of fate.

The émigrés often accuse the Bolsheviks of "distorting Marx," of not living "according to Marx." Of course, it is not so; but, in any case, why only Marx? The Bolsheviks are far greater sinners, for they do not even want to live "according to Darwin," and boldly strive to abolish humanity's struggle for existence, so as to apply all the energy which is absorbed by this struggle and which has now lost its meaning, to the struggle of man against nature, in order to subject its elemental forces to the rational interests of humanity.

And at the same time, the intellectuals abroad languish in melancholy and idleness, the remnants of their strength fast vanishing, and at heart regretting only one thing: the loss of those "evenings dear to the heart" when, sitting around a samovar, they waxed eloquent on the subject of the tyranny of autocracy, of their love for the people, and of the inconvenient way in which the universe as a whole is organised.

And it is likely that if Prometheus himself, having stolen some new fire to light up the secrets of life, appeared to them and interfered with their tea drinking, they would invoke their curses on Prometheus too.

1928

PHILISTINISM

A PHILISTINE is a person whose life is constricted by a narrow circle of habits and ideas acquired long ago, and who, within this circle, thinks automatically. The influence of family, school, church, "humanitarian" literature, of all that represents the "spirit of the law" and the "traditions" of the bourgeoisie, creates within the brain of the philistine a simple mechanism, similar to that of a clock, whose mainspring sets in motion the wheels of philistine ideas, a force that urges him continually towards a state of rest. The prayers of the philistine may, without damage to their eloquence, all be reduced to a few words: "God have mercy on me!"

As a demand on the state and society, this prayer, in a somewhat extended form, runs as follows: "Let me alone; let me live as I like!"

Every day the press reminds, and suggests to, the philistine that if he is an Englishman, he is the finest fellow on earth; or if he is a Frenchman, that he also is the finest fellow on earth. And, of course, similarly if he is a German or a Russian—he, too, is the finest fellow on earth.

In general, this supreme citizen of the "civilised" world is exactly like the savage who was asked by a missionary, "What would you like?"—and replied: "Little to do, little to think, lots to eat." The philistine is a pathological case: the technique of thinking, which has been so thoroughly acquired by man, prevents the growth of his mind. It sometimes happens that, under pressure of events, the philistine will acquire ideas that are alien to him; but they become a source of suffering to him, like eczema, or a stone in the kidney or the liver. In such cases he will often try to cure himself with anodynes, such as religion, pessimism, alcohol, debauchery, hooliganism, and so on.

To substantiate this, let me give an example. Eleven years ago, by the will of the Russian workers and peasants who had risen in revolt, the four years of wholesale slaughter of the people, engineered by the bosses of Europe for the sake of increasing their wealth, was brought to an end. The philistines had suffered very severely, both physically and economically, from the criminal and bloodthirsty game of the bankers and political adventurers. What effect did this suffering have on the "spiritual" life of the philistine, how did it alter the mechanism of philistine thought?

It had no effect whatever, it did not alter the accustomed mechanical operation of masculated thought in any way. The philistine remained convinced that religion is the foundation of morality and that the state could not exist without religion, although it had become perfectly obvious that the bourgeois state is immoral, that it is founded on theft, robbery, and the cynical exploitation of the working people. During the war they thought it perfectly natural to appeal for aid in their vile work of mutual extermination to their god, who had commanded them, "Thou shalt commit no murder," and "Love thy neighbour as thyself."

After the war the "humanitarianism" of the philistine remained just that "love of mankind," which consists in words and exists entirely outside of all reality, that it had been before the war. He is still able to shout a little in defence of personal liberty, but he is absolutely indifferent to the sufferings

47

and oppression of the masses. And, in general, the frightful lesson of the war in no way altered the psychology of the philistine, just as it did not alter the habits of mosquitoes, frogs, and cockroaches.

To-day the capitalist states of Europe are actively preparing for a new war. The military experts are of the unanimous opinion that the new war will be chiefly a chemical war, and that the destruction and horrors it will cause will infinitely exceed the destruction and horrors of the war of 1914-18. The Italian newspaper *Mattino*, in its issue of January 15, prints an article by Douhet, General Douhet, I think, a writer on military affairs, who quotes Admiral Bravetta as saying:

> Engineer-General Bourloen has calculated that, with the use of aeroplanes, 500 tons of phosgen gas are enough to completely contaminate within half an hour an area of 10,000 hectares, which is equivalent to the area of Paris.

Colonel Bloch states that:

> A phosgen bomb weighing 500 kilograms can penetrate a house and kill everybody in it. On exploding, such a bomb will form a cloud 100,000 cubic metres in volume, whose deadly effects will be instantaneous. A street 30 metres wide and 100 metres long would be contaminated to a height of 35 metres from the ground. Given a favourable (!) wind, all houses within a kilometre which are not hermetically sealed will be invaded by the gas.

General Fries, who is in charge of chemical supplies in the United States army, states that:

> A Lewisite bomb weighing 450 kilograms can render ten New York city blocks uninhabitable, and some hundred

tons of this splendid article can poison everything living and contaminate all water and food in New York for over a week.

Lord Nalsburg stated in the House of Lords, on July 11, that 40 tons of arsen could kill the whole population of London:

Means of biological warfare are also being developed. Search is being made for rapidly multiplying bacteria and the serum to combat them. Infected people will therefore have to beg for the serum as a cure, while the inventors of the serum will impose their own conditions on the people whom they have infected with, for instance, the plague.

The European press very often contains these and similar details about the future war. The European philistines read these articles, of course, and one would have thought they would understand that it is *their* children, wives, and old people who will be poisoned by these gases.

If a small group of thieves and bandits were to gather in one of the squares of London, Paris, or Berlin and publicly discuss which neighbourhood should be robbed first and the best way to rob it, the philistines, no doubt, would try by one means or another to frustrate the modest designs of these "socially-dangerous" citizens. But the philistines do nothing to prevent the incomparably more destructive designs of people incomparably more criminal and socially dangerous, who publicly discuss projects for the wholesale extermination of tens of millions of people.

Quite apart from "humanitarianism," one would have thought that the instincts of the property-owner and the promptings of self-defence would arouse alarm and terror in the hearts of the philistines. One would have thought that the philistine's natural gravitation towards a state of rest would make him cry out: "I don't want war!" But he does not.

When the Soviet government proposed a plan for immediate disarmament to the other powers, and then a plan for disarmament within four years, it seemed as though the philistine did not hear these proposals. He did hear them, of course, but the mechanical nature of his mind, circumscribed and repressed by the force of tradition, led him to regard this simple, clear and, in the fullest sense of the word, humanitarian proposal as something unrealisable and fantastic.

In his time the philistine has regarded many things as unrealisable and fantastic, *e.g.*, Fulton's steamboat, Yablochkin's electric lamp, and numerous other achievements of the free and daring mind, that force which creates culture and enriches life.

The chief motto of the philistine is: "As it has been, so shall it be." The sound of these words reminds us of the mechanical swing of a pendulum. The philistine is, indeed, degenerating. Like the fish, he is "rotting from the head down."

The philistine also regards as fantastic and impracticable the aim which the revolutionary-minded workers of the Soviet Union have set themselves, namely, to create a workers' state, free of exploiters and parasites.

The Soviet press, which is energetically "sweeping the rubbish out of the house," the rubbish that has accumulated for centuries, provides the philistine with an abundant supply of "spiritual food." And the philistine, battening on this rotten offal, livens up, smirks, winks to his friends, and whispers: "They won't succeed. We were right after all."

They have reason to rejoice: after all it is they who caused,

50

Philistinism

and continue to cause, all the litter and dirt. They have reason to rejoice: the refuse, the decayed rubbish, filth and all that the workers' and peasants' government is obliged to sweep out with an iron besom, is actually theirs, the philistines, by right, it is the product of centuries of their creative work.

In spite of his belief in the mercy of God and his certainty that the joys of paradise await him in the "life beyond," in spite of his hypocritical verbal "idealism," the philistine is a profound "materialist." And his first concern is for his economic welfare here on earth: "lots to eat, little to do, and little to think." That is why he whispers, mutters and groans: "There is a shortage of sugar; there is a shortage of eggs; there is a shortage of butter...."

He has forgotten, of course, that there has been shortage of everything ever since 1916, and that nearly all these foodstuffs disappeared during the years when the Whiteguard generals and the "spiritual leaders" of the philistines, in their endeavour to "save" Russia, were exterminating the working people and shattering their economic life. It would seem that the philistine is unaware that Napoleon's march on Moscow, for example, was mere child's play compared with the campaigns of Kornilov, Denikin, Kolchak, Wrangel, and all the other bestial patriots, who were inspired by the highly-cultured "patriots of their own estates" and the various "idealists" of private property. The fact that the economic life of the country, shattered by seven years of war, is being restored on a far wider scale and on more modern technical lines than before 1914 is something the philistine refuses to see. Indifferent to everything that does not affect him personally, and confined within his circle of accustomed values, he hisses: "There used to be more.... Now there is less." And he closes his eyes still

51

more tightly to the fact that, in the Soviet Union, the number of intelligent people and cultured workers who have risen from the ranks of the workers and peasants is rapidly growing. This fact is not at all to his advantage and, of course, he greets it with hostility.

The Russian philistine has been trained from yore to distrust and even to detest reason. The church was very zealous in seeing to that, and there were even writers who helped to foster this spirit. From the time of Gogol's *Correspondence* to our times, we find few important Russian writers who really appreciated the creative power of reason as it deserves to be appreciated in view of the tremendous services it has rendered to mankind. In 1851, Leo Tolstoy wrote in his *Diary*: "Consciousness is the greatest evil that can inflict man." Later, in a letter to Arseneva, he said: "A brain that is too large, is disgusting." His moral philosophy is thoroughly permeated by this conviction, and it finds reflection in his great literary works. Dostoyevsky, also, was at odds with reason; with his usual genius and skill he laid bare the overwhelming power of the irrational, the power of instinct. Leonid Andreyev regarded thought as the enemy of mankind; looking upon it, moreover, as a "sensual principle," as a special kind of emotion. One of the most talented of our modern writers puts the following words into the mouth of his hero: "Thought—there you have the source of suffering. Humanity will exalt the memory of the man who destroys thought."

Of course, an author is not responsible for the feelings, thoughts, and ideas of his characters, if he himself does not suggest them, does not impose his own feelings and thoughts —as L. Andreyev, for example, did—but objectively depicts the logical inevitability of the development of these thoughts and feelings, as Stendhal, Balzac, and Flaubert knew how to do so skilfully.

I am not speaking here of any particular author, but of a very essential fact, namely, that a hostile attitude towards thought finds expression at the very time when genuine and profound revolutionary thought, organising the will of the new class, is mastering life as rational activity, as labour and creation, as a process whose aim it is to thoroughly remould culture and life on the basis of collectivism. And side by side with this process, we clearly perceive a trend that is hostile to reason. In books written in a tone of respect, even of sympathy, for the Revolution, you sometimes perceive what is, perhaps, an involuntary and unconscious attempt on the part of the author to belittle the significance of thought, to depict it as impotent against the "super-rational" or "subconscious." If this is done well, it is instructive, and therefore useful. But there is evidently a law which prescribes that the vast majority of books should be bad books. In these books, thanks to the lack of technical skill of their makers, it is very easy to detect the influence of philistinism: it, too, emits, from its "insides" so to speak, a kind of poison gas—not very drastic in its action, perhaps, but nevertheless capable of poisoning people, especially young people.

There are many books which remind me of an old story. A bald man asks a man with long hair, "Why do you grow your hair so long?"—And the man with long hair replies: "Because my scalp, too, is naked underneath."

Not a very witty reply, perhaps, but a true one. There are people who cover themselves with a thick layer of revolutionary phrases, not because they want to conceal the nakedness of their scalps, but in order to hide, sometimes even from themselves, the hollowness of their own souls. It is probably in reference to books by such people, that a worker correspondent from the Donbas writes:

> You open the book and read a score or so of pages—deadly dull. The words are our words, but there is no pith to them. I have books like this, for instance: "A cloud of dust in the distance, the sound of horse bells, it is Alexander Zakharych coming." Now, in the village where I was born, in Lipetsk county, there used to be a village police inspector by the name of Alexander Zakharych, a jolly man and a drunk. He would take a drink with us young people, play a round of *gorodki,* then have another drink and begin to abuse the tsar,—and us, too. "The devil take you," he would say, "why don't you hurry up and start a revolt? As it is, it's neither one thing nor the other. We just live in a constant state of alarm." He wanted a constitution; he said that it would be easier, even for the tsar, under a constitution.

I have quoted this passage from the letter, not because it displays the interesting and imaginative mind of a working man, but in order to show that the masses are already beginning to develop a keen eye for insincerity in a book. This, of course, is nothing new; but it will do no harm to remember it. Yes, philistinism is growing and beginning to spread its wings, and more and more frequently one receives letters of complaint.

"It is hard to have to live in an atmosphere of philistinism triumphant"—this was written by a non-party woman, an old writer, and by no means the first among non-party people to feel that the philistines are making the atmosphere rather thick.

Philistinism

Another correspondent, also a non-party man, amusingly grumbles: "They have composed a hymn: they ask us to pity 'the private tradeswoman.' What fatuity!"

Gradually philistinism is acquiring its own literature, a literature which takes the philistine as its hero. This is managed very simply. The author takes some insignificant type, like Akakievich, from Gogol's *Greatcoat,* and endows him with the psychology of Ivan Ilyich, or of the hero of L. Andreyev's *Thought.* He then puts this synthetic character into a modern setting and so creates, as it were, a new character. The philistine reads this and gloats to himself: "These are just the sort of 'profound experiences' that may happen to me too." Our old friend Makar Devushkin, for instance, and many other "meek and offended ones," have been resurrected dozens of times already in new books. But it is not so much for Dostoyevskian reasons that they suffer; what worries them is the fact that "there is a shortage of molasses, eggs, and butter."

More and more frequently in modern literature, we find the "unique personality," so dear to the philistine's heart: the man who yearns for absolute freedom in order that he may manifest his own ego, and who wants to have nothing to do with the reality he despises. Having read a book whose hero has been patched together from bits and pieces stolen from our great writers, the modern philistine falls into a sort of holy adoration of himself and writes somebody a letter describing himself in the following terms:

"My whole career has been individual, unrepeatable, inimitable. Nobody else in the world or in life can repeat this career and go through the same stages, just as nobody has done so in the past."

If the writer confines the expression of his self-esteem to a letter, it is not so bad. But sometimes he will write a whole book, in which one finds such revelations as the following:

"... *My creative work was more intoxicating to me than wine, stronger than love, sweeter than sleep.*"

Not in the least perturbed by the dubious grammar of this sentence* he continues:

"*I cannot convince the sceptics, who consider the artist to be just an ordinary man, that at such moments, when I am intoxicated by the 'creative spirit,' I would become something higher than the ordinary man; everything is revealed to me. If only I were a legislator, I would pass a law granting the artist special privileges, so that he could rush from place to place by train and airplane, in order that his profound vision might penetrate the remote secrets of the world.*"

The author does not realise that this urgently expressed desire of his absurd hero—with whose transitory experiences and superficial views he sympathises—is both ridiculous and naïve. Nor do the critics. Authors are already beginning to regard themselves as "spiritual aristocrats," and generous publishers, who think that all this is as it should be, keep offering the reader larger and larger quantities of verbal chaff, while the critics, absorbed in mutual recriminations and in straightening out the ideological line, fail to observe that the "hundred per cent" philistine is worming his way into literature.

Lies may still exist, but only truth can attain perfection. Lies have entrenched themselves in the positions they occupied long ago; they are not developing, they are not increasing in subtlety, and their feeble fatuity is becoming more and more obvious. Fifty years have already elapsed since bourgeois thought created any new "systems of social philosophy,"

* In the Russian.—*Trans.*

systems that would assert in a way sufficiently convincing to the bourgeoisie, that it was created by nature, by God, and by history to rule the world. After Nietzsche's desperate, but unsuccessful, attempt to prove that life is senseless, that lies are essential, and that there is nothing unnatural or shameful in the fact that "men are wolves to one another," Spengler's book, *The Decline of the West,* and others like it, have frankly spoken of the exhaustion of the intellect and will of the bourgeoisie. They have established the fact that it is moving mechanically and of its own momentum towards complete degeneration.

There are many proofs of this, besides those adduced in *The Decline of the West.* Influences are making themselves felt in West-European literature that were formerly completely alien to it; for instance, Tolstoy, Dostoyevsky, and the often ridiculed Ibsen. His Nora, his Woman From the Sea, and other women characters are more and more becoming the heroines of English, French, and German novels and plays, and this testifies to the fact that the "foundation of the state," the solid bourgeois family, is being shaken. Writers in the West are more and more depicting the free woman, who boldly breaks with philistine tradition in order to lead an independent life. And this "emancipation" is real—not verbal: women are beginning to take charge of large business establishments, they go in for journalism and politics, and take part in hazardous adventures. In Germany, Eleonora Kuhn, a Doctor of Philosophy, advocates "gynecocracy," or the rule of women.

And alongside of this we find that sexual perversion is spreading. Homosexual "love" is more or less recognised as a natural thing; there are magazines devoted to it; "homosexual" clubs and restaurants exist legally; crime is spreading among the upper bourgeoisie, and so is suicide. All this we find calmly reported in the bourgeois press almost daily. And, in the same way as our own philistines are beginning to do, West-European writers construct their heroes from materials stolen from such literary masters and profound thinkers as Stendhal and Balzac, whose keen eye long ago detected the hypocrisy of bourgeois society. Moreover, one notes an increasingly critical attitude towards modern social conditions, a growth particularly to be observed among writers in the United States.

Truth is spreading and is perfecting itself; both the truth of science, which is rapidly helping the toiling people to gain mastery over the forces of nature, and the truth of the working masses' realisation of their social primacy, of their right to political power. The ancient social lie has no weapon against these two creative forces, which in the Soviet Union should, in the near future, merge into one; it has nothing to defend itself with except guns and gas—and the latter means philistine ideology, just as much as poison gas.

Philistine ideology and morality strive to bind as tightly as possible the will and reason of man, which are aiming towards collectivism. In our country, this morality is crumbling and disappearing. But it is a rough and painful process; for man has to combat not only his environment but also himself. This gives rise to a deplorable, but apparently inevitable, fact; namely, that people having one common aim, people who are comrades in their work for the future, nevertheless display a carelessness of each other's interests, a callousness, a mutual lack of appreciation of each other's merits, and a malicious, often heedless tendency to stress each other's shortcomings. People, though they are collectivists by conviction, often act all too individualistically in their personal relations with their comrades, especially with women. This, of course, derives from philistinism; it is one of its most painful legacies. But man cannot be expected to regenerate himself in ten years; he cannot forge a new morality, new "rules of conduct," in so short an interval.

However, it seems to me that it is already high time we began moulding a new bio-social hygiene, which may serve as the foundation of the new morality. The beginning of this process must be a deliberate effort to achieve a closer and more friendly unity among the people who are faced with the tremendous job of re-educating several scores of millions of small proprietors in order to make them cultured workers, conscious builders of the new state. It is scarcely necessary to insist that it is the duty of the critic and the journalist to undertake the development of this hygiene, this humanising of people; to wage a struggle against the resurrection of the poisonous philistine "ideology" and against all attempts to idolize the "meek and offended" philistines.

The hero of to-day is the man of the "masses," the handi-worker of culture, the rank-and-file Party member, the worker correspondent, the army correspondent, the village librarian, the promoted worker, the rural teacher, the young doctor and agronomist working in the countryside, the peasant "experimenter" and activist, the worker inventor, in a word—the man of the masses! And our chief attention must be devoted to the masses, to the training of such heroes among the masses.

It is rather embarrassing to have to mention this, but it seems to me to be necessary. Thousands of magazines, per-

Culture and the People

haps more, are being published in our country, and their number is growing. Quite a number of them have parallel aims and deal with similar material. Yet the great majority of these magazines are beyond the understanding of the general reader, for whom to this day there has not yet been written a "History of The Civil War" (which is absolutely essential), or a "History of The Development of the Social Estates in Russia" (which is no less essential). It is time to acquaint the ordinary reader, the masses, with the development of science and technology.

You cannot any longer educate people with skimpy pamphlets. They have become scornful of pamphlets, and demand "real books, something more solid." There are very few magazines for the general reader. What is provided by the *Workers' Newspaper* and the *Peasants' Newspaper* is, in my opinion, excellent; but something more is required. The rural population needs a magazine that will acquaint them with life in present-day Europe, with the life of the bourgeoisie, and which at the same time deals with the life of the working people. The masses need a great deal. I claim that too few books are being written for them. They do not need the dainty food of literary rhetoric; they need the filling bread of the truth, clearly and distinctly told, about the modern world, about the struggle of the working people for a brighter future in all countries.

By introducing the "column" feature, Comrade Zhiga has shown that he fully understands the general reader's demand for knowledge about life in the Soviet Union. Doubtless the "mechanical citizen" will not miss the opportunity of accusing me of "hostility to freedom of speech and personality," and to other sacred traditions. Yes, I *am* opposed to freedom—from the moment it becomes merely another name for license. And, as we know, this happens as soon as a man loses sight of his true social and cultural function and begins to give free rein to the ancient philistine individualism that is latent in him and to proclaim: "Here am I, so unique and inimitable, yet they won't allow me to live in my own way." And it is a good thing if he confines himself only to proclaiming it; for as soon as he begins to act in his own way he becomes, on the one hand, a counter-revolutionary and, on the other, a hooligan, which is almost equally vile and obnoxious.

Some comrades will probably be displeased by my reference to the multiplicity of learned Soviet magazines which are beyond the comprehension of the masses, and which, I think, are run at a fairly considerable loss. But what would you have? I am not the first to notice this fatty degeneration of periodical literature, nor am I the first to say that the masses are being supplied with literature all too unskilfully and ineffectually. I recall the lines:

> *Give us, GIZ,** more magazines,*
> *They multiply readers—*

But it does not seem to me that our magazines pay enough heed to the level of understanding of the general reader, or that they are capable of increasing his knowledge as they should.

What they do multiply are controversies; but even fairly educated people cannot always understand what they are about, and why Comrade Z fulminates at Comrade X as though he were an enemy, whence the strange and inappropriate tone of personal rancour both display, and why they so energeti-

---

* State Publishing House.—*Trans.*

cally scald each other with the boiling water of their self-esteem.

Why, in face of the enemy, must differences even of a terminological character be argued in forms which betray a lack of respect for each other on the part of the controversialists, as well as a lack of culture?

I have lying before me a number of books dealing with literary disputes. When the old Marxists entered into controversies with bourgeois critics and exposed their tendencies, they did so with a calmness that only made their articles more convincing. It cannot be said that our young critics, when "straightening out" each other's "ideological line," which fundamentally is quite straight and clear, follow this example. In their youthful impetuosity the critics forget that verbose eloquence often obscures the "fundamental line," and that their controversy itself is often beyond the understanding of the mass of young readers, especially in the provinces. We all too frequently hear complaints that literary criticism is "incomprehensible," "confused," and "contradictory."

"Over there, in Moscow, they talk a sort of family language, as though they were the only people in the world"—writes a literary "beginner" from the Urals. Another ironically remarks: "Each claims to be a most orthodox Marxist. They are all orthodox. Then why quarrel?"

I receive many such comments. One of them is characteristic:

> It is difficult for us, worker correspondents, to study dozens of articles. What we need is some sort of guide to the main points of literary history. We would then find it easier to understand subjective differences of opinion.

Philistinism

Would it not be more practical and useful if the critics were to decide their group differences and petty quarrels at conferences, and not in the columns of magazines, where articles written "in a state of annoyance and irritation" are often, in fact always, out of place? It seems to me that the summoning of small conferences of critics and writers for the comradely discussion of literary questions is something which in general the "spirit of the times" dictates.

1929

ANTI-SEMITISM

WASTREL is not merely a term of abuse: it is an exact definition of a man who is wasted to life. Under our conditions a wastrel is a creature who is profoundly and incurably infected with the diseases of the "old world": envy, greed, human hatred, and enmity of all that contradicts his habits and tastes and what he has retained from the old days, from the conditions of life under which "men are wolves to one another." This "legacy of the past" has become as deep-seated in the blood of the wastrel as syphilis and the craving for alcohol. Wastrels are therefore not only a social but a biological phenomenon. They have been produced and reared by the ruthless and bestial struggle for self-preservation, the "struggle for individual existence" that is natural and inevitable in a class state, where people are inevitably divided into slaves and masters, and where men must devour each other so as not to be devoured themselves.

A wastrel can only regard the "struggle for existence" as a struggle of man against man. As to the struggle of the collective will for mastery over the forces of nature in order to emancipate people from inhuman, senseless, and involuntary toil, the wastrel is constitutionally incapable of understanding it. He is just as accustomed to the methods and conditions of life of the old world as moles, marmots, and rats are accustomed to the conditions of their zoological life. The fundamental principle of the wastrel, his faith and spiritual world,

64

can be summed up in the simple words: "I want to fill my belly." Other people also want to eat, but this is something the wastrel is incapable of taking into account. He is a creature who is narrowly and preposterously restricted by his individual desires. To him the world is a place where people fill their bellies, and where he wants to fill his belly with more food and more tasty food than others. His whole will-power, his mind, and everything he calls his "spiritual urge," is directed towards this purely animal aim.

The other day some wastrels of the criminal family, that is to say, who commit villainies, sent me a leaflet entitled "Order to Communists," the authors of which, for reasons which will be easily understood, preferred to conceal their identity under the pseudonym "Communist Committee." This "Order" is written rather ungrammatically and very odiously. It calls upon Communists to start a Jewish pogrom. "Rise, you Russian people and all you nations—Tatars, Chuvashes, etc.—and kill the Jews!" This filthy document is nothing new to me, and, to tell the truth, does not in itself arouse my indignation. I have been fighting anti-Semitism to the best of my ability for thirty years, and I have read several score of such documents in my time. Nor do the wastrels themselves arouse any excessive indignation in me—for I am thoroughly convinced that they are doomed to extinction.

What does arouse my indignation, and very deeply, is something else, something more serious. I ask myself: How is it possible for such documents to appear in our country on the eve of the twelfth anniversary of the October Revolution? What sort of cultural environment is it, that allows in its midst such revolting villainy as anti-Semitism? Are we really to believe the spiteful assertions of the White émigré newspapers that Communists are also infected with anti-Semitism? Personally I am convinced that the authors of the leaflet are not Communists (for the Party knows how to sweep such garbage out of its ranks with a firm hand), and that they have only chosen the popular name of the Party in order to conceal their disgusting faces.

Nevertheless, I am perplexed by the strange fact: How is it possible in a country where, not merely in word but in actual deed national enmity is rejected by the whole political and cultural work of its dictators—the working class—and by the whole work of its brain—the Party—how is it possible in this country for anti-Semitism, that fatal expression of human hatred, to flare up so shamelessly and cynically?

There can be no question but that anti-Semites must be fought. But two questions arise: Are we fighting zealously enough; and how should the fight be waged?

In my opinion, the Russian people in the mass are not prone to anti-Semitism. This is eloquently borne out by many facts: for example, the "Subbotnik" (Sabbatarian) sect in the Kuban and on the Volga; the unchristened Jews, whom the peasants in certain parts of Siberia, elect as village elders; the attitude of Russian soldiers to Jewish soldiers; and so on. Moreover, what I have seen of the Jewish agricultural colonies in the Ekaterinoslav Province, and of the peasants of the Ukraine, enables me to affirm quite positively that the accusation of anti-Semitism cannot be levelled at the Russian people as a whole. The plunder of Jewish towns and villages and the wholesale murder of Jews were part of the system of the tsarist government. As we know, they were first applied on a large scale in the 'eighties. Alexander III once said to General Gurko: "You know, I get real pleasure when Jews are beaten up"! This is no anecdote, but the authentic words of a Russian emperor. It was a particular method of combating the "internal enemy." In the 'nineties the pogroms were repeated on an even wider, more cynical and atrocious scale. It should be borne in mind that the Romanov government kindled racial enmity which resulted in bloodthirsty massacres, not only between the Russians and Jews, but also between the Tatars and Armenians in the Caucasus.

But it was the Jews who were murdered and robbed most of all, because they were nearer, closer to hand, defenceless, and therefore could be beaten up more easily and comfortably. They were beaten up on the pretext of participation in the Russian revolutionary movement. I, personally, do not think that, in the struggle against the autocracy, the Jews played a bigger role than should have been played by Jewish workers and artisans stifled within the "pale" by restrictive laws and police tyranny.

When the tsarist government was in difficulty, it was nearly always the Jews who suffered most. I might mention the campaign against the Jews started by the disgraceful Beiliss trial. In 1915 the most shameful anti-Jewish propaganda was started in the army; all Jews in Poland and Galicia were declared the spies and enemies of Russia. A disgusting pogrom broke out in Molodechno. It has been established that this Jew-baiting originated at headquarters, and, of course, it could not but contribute to the disintegration of the army, in which there were about half a million Jews.

The people, enraged and blinded by want, were unable to detect their true enemy. If the authorities sanctioned the killing and robbery of Jews—why not kill and rob them? In the same way German shops in Moscow were also plundered during the war because it was suggested and sanctioned.

While the government, through the police, was engineering pogroms and doing nothing to prevent robbery and murder, people who were obviously abnormal used the press to disseminate hatred against the Jews. In Kiev this was done by a certain Shulgin, a journalist who, incidentally, definitely stated in his book *Days* that he also "hates His Majesty the Russian people." He was, as you can see, insane. In St. Petersburg the despicable propoganda of anti-Semitism was carried on by an important newspaper, Suvorin's *Novoye Vremya.* In Moscow the lawyer Shmakov, another degenerate type, was also active. Lastly, there was Dr. Dubrovin's monarchist organisation, which killed the well-known and talented journalist Yollos, and Gertzenstein. I, personally, always regarded the disseminators of racial and national enmity as degenerate and socially-dangerous people.

These are the conditions which produced and nurtured such characters as Petlyura.* His activities will be revealed in court by the documents; they are vivid and eloquent testimony to the blood-thirsty activities of the gang of brigands which he commanded. I have nothing to add to these documents, which I know to be authentic.

I am no defender of terrorism, but I cannot deny the right of a man to self-defence. It seems to me that a murder may be committed entirely from the fear that what has once been done may be repeated, and from the natural desire to prevent something more horrible than one's own moral death.

1929

* Ukrainian counter-revolutionary leader during the Civil War. Assassinated in 1926 by a Jewish immigrant in Paris.—*Trans.*

ON THE "GOOD LIFE"

THIS article is, as far as possible, a reply to the letters sent me by various correspondents during the past year. It is physically impossible for me to answer every letter. I do not reply—nor shall I do so—to letters from anti-Semites, counter-revolutionaries, and scoundrels in general. As I see it, a reply is due only to those young people who, as a result of a limited understanding of culture and a sense of irritation due to the buffets and pin-pricks of maladjusted conditions of life, make inordinate demands on present-day life, which it cannot yet satisfy.

I think these people are all right, but their longing for the certainty of a "good life," a life "all their own," makes them blind, and they fail to see, they do not understand, that the historic process which is developing in the Soviet Union is developing rapidly, in that very direction, the ordering of a "good life." But if my correspondents remain on the shifting sands of illiterate, irresponsible, individualistic carping criticism, where they are now standing, in danger of sinking up to their ears, if they cannot find the will power to get off this dead centre, then I think this "good" life will pass them by, will not be for them at all.

Our life would be easier, relations between people would be better, if people knew and remembered that there is no creative force in all the world other than the force of the human intellect, of the human will. The idea that other intellectual forces exist outside of man originated in the primitive chaos of nature, when the intellect was negligibly equipped with experience and, therefore, was itself negligible. At that time, if a rock broke off a mountainside and rolled to the bottom, man did not understand what force set the rock in motion. He believed that all kinds and forms of motion were caused, on and above the earth, by forces which it was not for him to understand. Terrified by some phenomena of nature, encouraged by others, he defied everything he could not understand. He even made a god of death, the force which stops all motion visible to the eye. Some of my correspondents philosophize on the "be-all and end-all": love and death; they are particularly worried by death, which "bars the path of all that lives."

I have been on very close terms with at least a score of fairly intelligent people, who thought that ruminating on death made them more intelligent. I have heard them with mixed feelings, but I must say frankly, that the most charitable feeling I entertained for these philosophers was one of regret for the time they were wasting in attempts to light up the darkness with the stars people see when they run their heads against a stone wall.

I think that the "passion for speculative labour" in this direction blunts the "perceptive faculty" and leads the speculator into a dark corner, where the young philosopher, much to his own surprise, arrives at the inference: "I have finished writing, yet it seems to have been written not by me, a Young Communist League member and Marxist, but by somebody else, the devil knows who."

I think people should philosophize, not "speculatively," but discreetly, not from books, but by relying on the facts within personal experience, relying on the wealth of material provided by the reality in which the "great cause of our age" is developing, in which a "new world" is being built. Furthermore people should know and remember that this reality takes time, periods predetermined for it by history, and that in the realm of the "philosophical" a very great deal has been prudently provided just for the purpose of hindering the development of the "great cause of our age."

If young people start thinking that, in half a century, they will have to exchange their place on earth for one under it,— "into the gloom and chill of the void" or "somewhere,"—as they write—it means that these fellows are leaving life already. And since life is jealous and is no patron of loafers, youngsters must not be offended if it bundles them into the debris of metaphysics by the scruff of the neck. Life, in spite of its outward deformities inflicted by the wrongdoings of men, is biologically healthy, full-blooded; it requires the strong, the bold, and it sweeps self-abusers and word-abusers ruthlessly aside.

It seems to me that of all philosophical "systems of appraising the mutual relations between man and the world," the best and truest is the one which is yet to come, but is being formed. I have no idea what it will be like, and to guess about it is not my business.

I shall not speak of "love." However, I shall remark that in the sphere of sexual relations the young generation, in my opinion, is guilty of an over-simplicity which, sooner or later, the culprits will have to pay for dearly. It is my sincere wish that the day of reckoning for the grossness and ignominy of this over-simplicity should come as soon as possible.

And here, by the way, I should just like to say a word about dogs. It is all very well to learn friendliness to man from dogs, but people should not imitate their four-footed friends in anything else.

Like all the phenomena of our world, death is a fact which should be studied. Science is studying it more and more closely and diligently; and to study is to master.

Life has something to thank death for—it destroys everything that is played out, everything that has outlived itself and become mere ballast on the earth. People will point out that death does not spare children, a force which is yet undeveloped, and often destroys adults, who have not yet exhausted their powers. Often people with remarkable gifts and of value to society die in their youth, while mediocrities and jackasses live to a ripe old age; parrots, for instance, live to be a hundred and over. All this is true. But these melancholy facts are by no means due to the "blind, elemental, invincible power of death," but to unhealthy and abominable conditions of a social and economic nature. The cause of the premature death of socially valuable people is usually physical exhaustion, which, in its turn, is a result of the rapacious "proprietary" attitude which looks upon man as mere labour power, which should be "used up" quickly before another proprietor gets hold of it. It is a well-known fact that tens of thousands of manual workers and clerical workers are worn out before their time, and perish, from a basely cynical and, very often, stupidly intense exploitation of their powers.

People die of cholera, typhus, malaria, tuberculosis, plague, etc. But, after all, there is no reason why the germs of these diseases should exist in "cultured states." There is no reason why, around magnificent cities, there should be dense rings of squalid suburbs, where the houses are packed with people as cess-pits are with garbage. Luxurious hotels are not so socially important as good hospitals. It is tiresome having to repeat such elementary axioms but, apparently, this has to be done in the interests of illiterate people.

The adherents and advocates of the "civilised" rule of the capitalists have to persuade themselves that, if a louse bites them on the backside, neither the louse nor the backside is to blame, but a "law of nature." On the contrary, it is precisely this same philistine backside, which is used to a quiet, comfortable, and soft seat, that we must blame, because it has created, and preserves, the conditions which make for the existence of lice, fleas, microbes, poverty, squalor, illiteracy, superstitions, prejudices, and everything that afflicts the world of the labouring poor, who work day and night for the comfort of the philistine's backside.

Now, in the Soviet Union, we have only just begun to improve the social conditions for the bringing-up of children and the protection of motherhood; yet child mortality has already fallen, and is still declining. And, thanks to the system of vacations, thanks to rest homes, etc., the health of the workers is improving.

We know that "civilised states" are very large-hearted when it comes to funds for the manufacture of arms, guns, tanks, aeroplanes, explosives, poison gas, and everything intended for the wholesale destruction of human beings. The cost of homicide is rising all the time, swallowing thousands of tons of gold won by the workers, collected in the form of taxes from people who will be shot, blown up, gassed, and drowned in the sea for their pains.

The manufacturers of cannon, machine guns, dynamite, mustard gas, and other charming things designed for wholesale murder, are preparing for a future world carnage no less

earnestly—but, of course, more substantially and rationally—
than the medieval barons of Europe, who, deciding to plunder
the Orient, prepared for the conquest of Jerusalem and the
"delivery of the holy sepulchre." The difference is that, for
the modern "knights without fear and without reproach,"
Jerusalem lies in the city streets, where the banks are concentrated, and the "holy sepulchre" in safes.

This is work for death; this is a proper subject for the attention and philosophical interest of young people who are hyper-
sensitive to the discomforts of life in the Soviet Union, of a
life which is only in the initial stages of its construction along
new lines. I think that the awareness of personal discomfort,
of irritation, and other troubles is too morbidly developed in
many youngsters. This is a bad sign, it is a sign of a poorly
developed vitality. Life needs people who are strong and
hardy.

But death is not an evil in that it strikes down people who
have not lived till their powers are exhausted by the business of life: in this respect people can limit its power and operation, by being more attentive to and careful of each other,
by beginning to spend money more generously on health protection, hygiene, sanitation, and research into the causes of
disease. Science has vanquished small-pox, cholera, diphtheria,
the plague—epidemic diseases through which, in the past, tens
of thousands of people died untimely deaths. In their struggle
against death, medical men are becoming more and more
experienced and successful.

Death is an evil in that it strikes fear into men and makes
some of them spend their valuable energies on a "speculative,"
philosophical investigation into the "secret of death." But
philosophy never invented even a mustard plaster, and mus-

tard plasters and castor oil are much more useful in the fight against death than the philosophy of Schopenhauer or E. Hartmann.

Death is an evil in that, from fear of it, the human imagination has created gods, the "other world," and wretched fictions like Paradise and Hell. But we have long reached the stage where our "mortal" men—mining engineers, miners, smiths—are more skilful than Vulcan the god of the underworld; and electrical engineers are much more powerful, are of much more use to life, than Jupiter, the former lord of thunder and lightning.

The "other world" lies in the dark region of our emotions, which still differ all too little from the emotions of primitive man, because in them fear of death predominates, together with the chaotic operation of the "instinct of propagation," the unreasoning impulse to which is also excited by the fear of death. If the "other world" exists somewhere in the universe, we shall probably discover it, having first established interplanetary communication in our own solar system and then communication between worlds. But we can afford to take our time with this: first of all let us think about putting our life on earth into good order.

Is it necessary to insist that Paradise is one of the crass fictions, invented by high-priests and "fathers of the church," a fiction whose purpose it is to requite the hellish torments of people on earth with the soap bubble of a hope of peace in another place? Besides, the idea behind it is that the dream of heavenly bliss may to some extent obscure, and even extinguish, in the eyes of the poor, the alluring, rainbow lustre of the life of the rich here on earth.

Death is an evil in that religions were founded on the fear

75

of it. At the beginning of the conscious life of primitive men, when religious lore was their attempt to organise the chaos of natural phenomena, and embody these phenomena in the idea of semi-human gods, this folklore, which contained no element of intimidation, had a certain social value; it promoted the development of thought, fantasy, and imagination, and it still retains its value as "art."

But the high-priests and clergy, having destroyed religious lore as an art, constructed from the religious ideas of the people systems of morality, which were based on intimidation. Thus for a long time they held back the free development of thought, the knowledge of nature, and all fantasy and imagination.

Especially fatal to the growth of culture was the influence of Christianity which filled the world with the demons into which it transformed the ancient deities, half-gods and half men. It was Christianity that produced tens of thousands of ignorant monks who, in their dread of the power of the demons, exhorted men to renounce the world and infected them with dark superstitions, while those whose ideas strove against the fanatical asceticism and stultifying tyranny of the church were denounced as men possessed, heretics, wizards, witches, and were burnt at the stake. It was Christianity, and no other religion that hatched the idea of a "Holy Inquisition" which, operating for nearly seven hundred years, burnt hundreds of thousands of "heretics" and "witches" at the stake, and inflicted less severe punishments on several hundreds of thousands of others. In spite of the boasted "humanism" of Christianity, the Inquisition was abolished by Napoleon Bonaparte in Spain only in 1800 and in Italy in 1808; and even so, attempts were later made to restore it. The fanatical, ruthless struggle of the Christian church against science—the worst blot on the history of Europe—has yet to be adequately elucidated. The moral savagery of civilised people, inculcated by the church, is seen best of all from this fact: that during the bloody imperialist war the Christian-Germans prayed, "God, punish England." Yet in the same strain, to the same God, the "God of mercy," the British, French, and Russians also prayed for succour in their homicidal cause.

I hope that in reply to the questions of some of my correspondents with regard to the "merit," to the "necessity" of religion, to "religion as the foundation of worldly morality," and, ultimately, as a "consolation," I have made myself plain enough. As regards "consolation," I am quite sure that intelligent labour is a man's fullest consolation. At least, everything in our world is made simple, all problems and secrets are solved, only by the labour and creativeness of man, by his will and the power of his mind. Whereas everything is only complicated and obscured by the "mischievous philosophising" of wiseacres, who seek to justify the shame of modern life and reconcile people to it.

It is time we admitted that the only intellectual force that exists in the world is the human mind, that our mundane world and all our ideas about the universe have been organised, and are organised, only by our intellect. Outside its influence there are the movements of glaciers, hurricanes, earthquakes, droughts, impassable swamps, thick forests, sterile deserts, wild animals, snakes, parasites. All that exists outside of man is chaos and an infinite void filled with a chaos of stars, a chaos into which the mind of man, his instinct of knowledge, has introduced and is introducing harmonious order, just as successfully as he is putting the earth in order, draining swamps, irrigating deserts, cutting roads through mountains, destroying beasts of prey and parasites, "tidying up" his globe like a good housekeeper.

It is also possible that we have not as yet a sufficiently clear grasp of the essence of the forces of nature. But we are no longer subject to them; we rule over them and they serve us obediently. If this cannot "console" the pessimists, all that remains for their consolation is the logical and practical conclusion from their feeling of mistrust in the powers of culture—their loathing of life. The history of culture tells us that the knowledge won by the labour of men, amassed by science, is continually increasing, is becoming deeper, wider, more penetrating, and serves as a fulcrum for further progress in the endless development of our perceptive faculties and creative powers. Hence it follows that, if culture is to develop rapidly and fruitfully, we must have a good knowledge of its history.

The people whose letters I am answering have either a poor knowledge of the past or none at all, or else they do not want to have any: an indifference which points definitely to an extremely low ebb of the will to live. People who say that "men lived easier and freer in the past," that "Tolstoy was right when he denied culture," "that books lead only to pride," that "Gogol began with self-criticism and came to God for all that," —all these people are, from my point of view, abnormal, unhealthy. Their number seems to be growing, although this may only seem so because their complaints are growing more morbid and noisy. All these complaints indicate a convulsive attack of individualism, and they are all aptly formulated in a letter from a peasant or petty bourgeois of the town of Nizhnedevitsk: "In the collective farms, I realise, there is no freedom for my free soul. I should do better to become a tramp than to join one."

This man has no "free soul," and never could have had one, because from time immemorial man has been living in conflict with man, not for man and against nature. There is nothing new in this very simple thought, but the seeming naïveté of some thoughts indicates their sterling veracity. A man whose life is spent in the constant exertion of all his energies and faculties in self-defence against other men, cannot be as free within himself as he ought to be. The social conditions which leave man only three alternatives—either as the oppressor, or as the oppressed, or as the reconciler of unreconcilables— must once and for all be abolished.

Everything which, in one way or another—whether in the form of physical obstacles arising from nature or the class structure of the state, or in the form of "ideological" violence, such as that of the church—hinders the free development of human powers and faculties, and the process of culture, must be abolished. In this direction a good start has already been made by the working class, and it is precisely the success of this start that is causing individualism to have such agonising convulsions.

It cannot be denied that individual initiative has given, and is still giving, brilliant results in various spheres of science, technology, and art. This is, and has been, the case where this initiative coincides closely with the general trend of the "traditions," tastes, and interests of the ruling class—the bourgeoisie.

But whenever an individual has gone against the interests, habits, thought, and "tradition" of world philistinism, there has been no place for it—the individual has been exiled, gaoled, or burned at the stake. The fate of Socrates and Galileo has overtaken tens and hundreds of people, who have tried to shake the rigid foundations of life and thought. In this persecution of recalcitrants—therefore "good-for-nothings"—world philistinism reveals with the utmost frankness the depth of that duplicity, which it finds to be essential to it as a method of defending itself and tightening its grip on the world it dominates.

We know that philistinism, by its very thoughts and feelings, is profoundly individualistic. It cannot help this because its individualism has been formed by the "sacred institution of private property," the root principle of philistine society. The aim of all and every philistine philosophy is to reinforce and justify this principle as the only one that allegedly leads people along the path "to brotherhood, equality, freedom," and to the "peaceful collaboration of classes."

The falsity of this philosophy has been convincingly exposed by the teachings of Marx. It has been proved by facts like the European war of 1914-18; like fascism, which was allowed to develop and still is developing; by the inadequate state of organisation of the working class of Europe, which is strongly infected with the poison of philistine influences.

The duplicity and falsity of philistine individualism are shown quite plainly in its attitude to an individual member of society. In every way, philistinism holds back and deforms the normal development of individual powers and faculties. The growth of individuality in class society is limited by a complex system of oppression in the interests of nation and class, a system of religious and philosophical ideas and "legal" conceptions. The purpose of this system is to develop in man the characteristics of a "social animal," but it achieves the opposite effect: it educates the majority of people as mere domestic animals for the minority; and for the minority of emotionally powerful personalities it facilitates the ways and means of oppressing the majority.

The activity of the strong is manifested for the most part in a rapacious accumulation of capital, that is to say, in legalized robbery, or else in crimes against society, penal offences, such as petty larceny, gangsterism, and murder, and in sexual licence.

In the case of those who are not so strong, the pressure of the system of class tyranny, acting on their emotions, on the "subconscious," causes a general perplexity and fear of life. It makes such people think just as our primitive ancestors, those creators of all gods and religions, used to think, that there exist, outside of man, spiritual forces hostile to him and insuperable.

In other cases, the emotions are so irritated by the contradictions of life that they arrest, and obscure, the growth of consciousness. But this does not prevent such people from thinking that their "consciousness has already defined the process of being"; and such a frame of mind deepens still more the breach between man and reality, turning him into an anarchist and leading him to make such absurdly malicious remarks as the following:

"Life has been playing cat-and-mouse with me ever since I was fifteen, and now I hate everyone who tries to educate the people. I am cleverer than such folks, and I regret very much that I defended them at the front with a rifle in my hand, without sparing myself."

This is the cry of a man who has already gone mad in the fruitless struggle "for one's self."

Culture and the People

The class system of the capitalist state divides people into the oppressors, the oppressed, and the reconcilers of the irreconcilable—this was proved so long ago and so irrefutably that it is almost unnecessary to mention it. However, we cannot help mentioning it because, in their frantic hurry to achieve a comfortable place in life, many young people, we are sure, do not realise that their haste will drag them back into the past—into that tragic circus, where capitalist reality rages so hideously and cynically, and where the humanists and conciliators play the part of lyrical clowns.

The famous mathematician, Einstein, is recognised by scientists the world over as a man of genius. It is reasonable to suppose, therefore, that he fully understands contemporary events. Well, there is an article by him in the English *Sunday Dispatch,* in which, incidentally, is the following estimate of Bolshevism:

"Bolshevism is an amazing experiment. It is not impossible that the trend of the social revolution will be in the direction of communism. The Bolshevik experiment was worth making."

The main trend of modern history is against individualism, and is towards the transformation of life on collective, socialist principles. This is not an "invention of the Bolsheviks," it is the natural, logical result of the development of general human culture. The "Bolsheviks" were brought forth by history, they are its "legitimate" children; it created them, reared them, and advanced them to the first place as organisers and leaders of the masses, the workers and peasants.

The past has made it sufficiently plain to us that zoological, animal individualism—the basis of small private economy—served and still serves as a polluted, putrescent soil for the development of parasites and extortioners brutalised by an in-

82

sane passion for profit, who for the sake of gain are capable of destroying tens of millions of workers and peasants in war and who daily destroy tens of thousands by inordinate overwork, by malnutrition, hunger, and disease.

The Party—the brain of the working class—created by the genius of Vladimir Ilyich and the energy of his comrades, has undertaken a task of unparalleled, of colossal, difficulty: it is building a socialist society of people who are really equal.

The conditions under which it carried out, and is still carrying out, its work are as follows:

human material, talented by nature, but poorly educated or quite illiterate, profoundly uncultured, profoundly anarchised by the Romanov autocracy and Russian capitalism, which was monstrously uncivilised;

a peasantry—eighty-five per cent of the population—inured for centuries to "thresh rye for bread with an axe's head," to "eat their stew with a wooden shoe," crushed by a poverty-stricken existence and hard labour, superstitious, intemperate, completely ruined first by an imperialist, and then by a civil war, a peasantry which even now after ten years under the revolutionary influence of the town, still retains, in the majority, the psychology of the small proprietor, the psychology of the blind mole;

a long-winded, weak-kneed intelligentsia, which for a hundred years had been solving questions of "social etiquette," which met the October Revolution with passive sabotage or with active, armed resistance, and which often continues to struggle "in word and deed" against Soviet rule, even up to the present day, committing conscious and unconscious sabotage;

the small townsfolk of a host of provincial towns, an army of abject slaves to capital, an army of marauders whose thievish custom it was to fleece the workers and peasants;

mills and factories, wretchedly equipped, and half-wrecked by the civil war in the bargain; a complete lack of factories for the production of heavy machinery;

dependence on foreign capital, though with an untold abundance of raw material, which the capitalists, in their anxiety to make quick millions, had not learned to manufacture, preferring to plunder and squander the people's estate;

a vast country with a negligible number of railways, with wrecked bridges, shattered rolling stock, a country with no highroads to connect it;

and over and above this, the active, unabating and blackguardly hatred of the world bourgeoisie—

Such is the tally, and by no means a complete one, of the heavy heritage which fell to the working class and its Party.

Furthermore, there are still some people who lived so serenely and cosily yesterday, that the cultural achievements of to-day give rise to nothing but a foxy or wolfish hostility, in that organ which they are pleased to call their "soul." For them, of course, it would be much more agreeable if the new state of affairs were a hundred per cent worse than it is, because in their eyes "the better, the worse." And there are other people, so well polished by the past, that the facts of the present slip over their tongues, without touching either their mind or their heart.

Finally we must add a very substantial number of dolts, loafers, "grafters," two-faced "friends of the proletariat," and other such parasites on the proletariat.

On the "Good Life"

It is under such conditions, with such people, on a soil swamped by ancient slime, mud, and putrescence, that the Soviet government has commenced its work and has already achieved a progress that is obvious, indisputable, and amazing.

"Our life is becoming more and more cruel," I am informed by "Two," who formulate in these words the complaints of many others. The people who say these things have a poor knowledge of the past, but it may be true, because it is the Party's duty to act, and it does act, with all the decision necessary for the leader of an army surrounded by enemies, a leader firmly convinced that the soldiers of the army are strong enough to beat the enemy.

By some strange chance the bulk of the opinions, reproaches, and complaints of my correspondents are often illiterate. One can hardly put this down to youth: pioneers are younger, yet their social literacy seems to be emotionally higher than that of people who have turned twenty. Sometimes one or other of these fault-finders appears to be "playing the fool." For instance:

"Workers should overcome the class psychology in themselves, first of all."

In other words: the working class should disarm ideologically. This is so stupid that it is not even surprising. It is noteworthy that not one of these correspondents says that the working class must rid itself of the philistine habits and tastes, abandon the philistine psychology, which are still part of its nature.

Very often complaints are made that places cannot be found in the universities. "We are not allowed to learn," they write. This is not quite true. It would be more correct to say that

85

a good many workers' children, too, lack the opportunity to get into universities, and they must all study. This is necessary just because there is a danger that children of the other classes, after passing through the university, will start life as "intellectuals," and then, following in the footsteps of their grandfathers and fathers, will again take up the "good cause" of reconciling irreconcilables, will begin to settle questions of "social etiquette," and in general "start day-dreaming" about how nice it would be if only people became "sensible and kind." This is to take the optimistic view but, of course, the result might be much worse. My correspondents ought to understand that they are living in years of war and that it is hypocritical and stupid to demand "mercy" on the battlefield during the fighting.

Probably, when there is no longer a single slave, a single loser, left in the world, man will be ideally good, but if there are to be no losers and no slaves, it is necessary to fight ruthlessly against the people who are accustomed to living on the labour of slaves.

People have been taught for two thousand years and more, that men should be meek and mild. But the preaching of humanism has long ago shown its utter futility. Nothing could have been more enthusiastic than the reception which the Christians of civilised Europe in the nineteenth century gave to Friedrich Nietzsche, who sincerely hated any humanity as a sign of weakness in the commanding class.

"Blessed are the meek, for they shall inherit the earth," says the Gospel. In Mark Twain's opinion this was said for the benefit of the English capitalists, who have really left behind them a trail of blood and violence in all countries of the world. No, we had better not talk of humanism while capitalism is

On the "Good Life"

still alive and is carefully preparing a new world carnage. Moreover, "war breeds heroes" and "heroes are the adornment of mankind." Yes, mankind has been prettily adorned with the real heroes of the war of 1914-18, the profiteers of all nations—the *"schieber,"* the *"nouveaux riches,"* and the "sharks." These people who having sucked enormous riches from the blood of the workers and peasants and continuing to control the power and will of the working masses in the same calm way, are organising fascism, the old, medieval form of tyranny, in order to tighten their hold. And the working class is "humanely" putting up with it all, risking a temporary reversion to the bloody gloom of the Middle Ages.

If my correspondents, and Soviet citizens in general, had ever awakened one fine morning convinced that the cause of the working class is really the "greatest cause of our age," if they could objectively appraise all that has already been built by the will of the workers of the Soviet Union, and all that is being built, they would feel all the better for it. It would probably give them the strength to work "not from fear, but for conscience's sake."

But beliefs are made not in dreams, but by cold reality. This reality will be less and less charitable to people who see and feel nothing in life but themselves, have no power of observation, do not want to learn anything and, not knowing the least thing about the past, cannot understand the great value of the present, do not feel that the principal purpose of the creativeness of the working class, the aim of its best, most rational, and healthiest energy is—in the long run—the complete emancipation of man.

Karl Marx reduced all "truths" to one specific truth, which

87

must be brought about by the new historical force, the working class. He said:

"The supreme being for man is man himself. Consequently, all relations, all conditions in which man is a humiliated, enslaved, despised creature, must be destroyed."

1929

IF THE ENEMY DOES NOT SURRENDER HE MUST BE DESTROYED

ORGANISED by the teachings of Marx and Lenin, the energy of the vanguard of the workers and peasants is leading the masses of the Soviet Union toward a goal whose significance is expressed in five simple words: to create a new world. In the Union of Soviets even Young Pioneers understand that if a new world and new conditions of life are to be created, it must be made impossible for individuals to accumulate, in any way whatsoever, tremendous riches, such as have always been squeezed out of the blood and sweat of the workers and peasants.

It is necessary to abolish the division of people into classes; to abolish every possibility of a minority exploiting the labour and creative power of the majority. It is necessary to expose the poisonous falsehoods of religious and national prejudices, which separate people, making them incomprehensible and alien to each other; to burn out of the life of the toilers all the filthy and savage customs of their every-day life, bred by age-old slavery; to destroy everything which hinders the growth of consciousness of the unity of their vital interests, and which allows the capitalists to cause the slaughter of human beings, to set millions of toilers against each other in war—always with the same object, of strengthening the right of the capitalists to rob the people, of increasing their senseless thirst for profit and their power over the workers.

Culture and the People

It means, in the long run, creating the conditions for the free development of the gifts and abilities of the whole people and of each individual; it means creating equal opportunity for the whole people so that every one may reach a level to which, so far, only the exceptional, the so-called "great" people, have been able to attain, and then only at the expense of a tremendous amount of wasted energy.

Is this the dream of a romantic? No, it is a reality. It is only the enemies of the workers and peasants who call their mass movement towards the building of a new world "a romantic dream." As "A Russian Woman" wrote to me not long ago, they are "a thin layer of well-educated people, with European minds," who, as she writes, are convinced that "intellect belongs to the few," that "one should not look for intellect among the masses"; that "culture was created by a few highly talented people."

In these words "A Russian Woman" harshly, but truly, expressed the whole significance of bourgeois ideology and its poverty; she revealed all that the bourgeois mind opposes to the spiritual regeneration of the proletarian masses. This spiritual regeneration of the proletariat throughout the world is an incontestable reality. The working class of the Soviet Union, marching at the head of the proletarians of the world, splendidly confirms this new reality. It has set before itself a great task, and its concentrated energy is successfully accomplishing it. The difficulties are tremendous but, when one really desires, one can achieve!

Already in the first years of its dictatorship, the working class, almost unarmed, barefoot, in rags, starving, threw out of the country the Whiteguard armies, excellently equipped by the capitalists of Europe, threw out of the country the troops of the interventionist powers.

For thirteen years the working class has been building its own state, with the assistance of a small number of honest, sincerely devoted specialists, but against the opposition of a multitude of vile traitors, who disgustingly compromise their comrades and even science itself. Working in an atmosphere poisoned by the hatred of the world bourgeoisie, amid the snake-like hissing of the "mechanical citizens," who greet every small mistake, every defect, every sin with malicious joy; working in these hellish conditions, whose burden and horror it does not yet fully realise, the working class has developed a truly amazing, a genuinely revolutionary and wonderful energy.

Under such conditions, only the heroic courage of the workers and of the Communist Party—which represents the intellect of the working class, the mind of the revolutionary masses—is able to perform such exploits as, for instance, raising the output of industry by twenty-five per cent, instead of the twenty-two per cent called for by the 1929-30 Plan. Collective farmers were scheduled to till twenty million hectares; they actually tilled thirty-six million! At the same time, the working class and the peasants, employing their energy in building up industry, in reorganising the countryside, have produced hundreds of talented workers, shock workers, worker-correspondents, writers, inventors,—their own, new intellectual forces.

From within the country, cunning enemies organise a shortage of food. The kulaks terrorise the collective farm peasants by murder, by arson, by all sorts of villainies; everything that has outlived the term set by history is against us, and this gives

91

us the right to consider ourselves as being still in a state of civil war. The natural conclusion which follows is: *"If the enemy does not surrender, he must be destroyed.*

Outside our country, European capital is against us. It also has outlived its time and is doomed to destruction. But it still wants to, and has the power to, resist the inevitable. It works hand in glove with those traitors who carry on wrecking inside the Soviet Union, and they, to the limit of their baseness, help its thieving aims.

Poincaré—one of the leading organisers of the European slaughter of 1914-18, nicknamed Poincaré "la-guerre," a man who almost destroyed the game of the French capitalists,—the former Socialist Briand, the notorious Lord Birkenhead, and other loyal lackeys of capital, are preparing, with the blessing of the head of the Christian church, a brigand attack on the Soviet Union.

We live in a state of constant warfare against the bourgeoisie of the whole world. This obliges the working class to prepare actively for self-defence and for the defence of everything it has created, both for itself and as an example for the proletarians of the whole world.

The working class and the peasantry must arm themselves, bearing in mind that once already the Red Army has triumphantly withstood the attack of world capitalism. Then, the Red Army was unarmed, starving, barefoot, in rags; it was led by comrades not very well trained in military science. Now, we have a Red Army, an army of fighters, and every fighter knows well what he has to fight for.

If, through fear of the inevitable future, the capitalists of Europe go completely mad, and dare to send their workers and peasants against us, we must be prepared to meet them with such deeds and words as will strike off the head of capitalism once and for all and throw it into the grave that history has already prepared for it.

1930

"THE PEOPLE MUST KNOW
THEIR HISTORY!"

THESE words were often repeated by the liberal "educators of the people" long before the October Revolution. They expressed the desire of the Russian bourgeois intellectuals to equip the working people with a knowledge of their past and rouse them to active opposition against the autocratic order of the Romanov tsars. For these autocrats were reluctant to share the "fullness of their power" with the landowners, manufacturers, and bankers. In the states of Western Europe the capitalists had long ago taken over power from the monarchy and made themselves complete masters of the soil and the lives of the people—the same people, of course, through whom they had seized power.

What did the workers and peasants gain when power passed from the kings and nobles to the bankers and manufacturers? Real life to-day gives the answer: among the capitalists of Europe the lust for profit has become a meaningless, mechanical habit, the savage sweating of labour-power from the workers has led capitalism into an unparalleled economic crisis, over thirty million workers have been thrown on the streets to starve, while the capitalists, exploiting the defencelessness of working folk, are cutting the wages of those still in employment.

"The people must know their history." Before the October

The People Must Know

Revolution the masses could not know their history for the very simple reason that almost all the workers and peasants were nearly or completely illiterate. But even if this reason had suddenly, by some miracle, been eliminated, the working people would still not have learned the real historical truth about their past. They would have remained ignorant of it, not only because knowledge of the truth was strictly forbidden by the tsarist censors, not only because in addition to the censorship special branches of the police and secret service were keenly on the watch to keep the truth from the rank and file of the labouring class; they would have remained ignorant of the truth because the truth was damaging and dangerous to the landowners, manufacturers, bankers. The genuine, incontestable truth of history is, that the whole life of the workers and peasants is nothing but a struggle of people without arms, education, or rights against people armed with all the knowledge of science, and holding absolute rights to plunder other men's labour.

"The people must know their history." What would a true history of their past life have told them?

They would have learned from the telling of it that their intellect and their will played no part in the process of history, that their whole lives only accomplished their own enslavement to the selfish, inhuman will of the capitalists. They would have learned that in various countries from time to time the people could no longer endure their slavery; and then from their midst, from their own flesh and blood, sprang the organisers of their wrath and vengeance. Then came the Italian, Fra Dolcino; the German, Thomas Munzer; the Czech, John Huss; then came the Russians: Ivan Bolotnikov, Stepan Razin, Yemelyan Pugachev. All these insurrections suffered the same fate:

the soldiery of the church, the kings, the tsars—peasants themselves, the well armed serfs of the boyars and nobles, drowned
the insurrections in the blood of their brothers; the leaders
were butchered by executioners, while the survivors of the
defeat once more fell into the power of the boyars, nobles,
kings, and tsars.

History would have told them how half-literate priests taught
the working people patience and submission to the "authorities
appointed by God"; how peasants were made monks by force
and monasteries built with their man-power; how the number
of "lay parasites" was swollen and brought into being, in which
the peasant worked with a plough and his parasite with a
spoon. To increase its power and influence over the ignorant
people, the church staged flimsy tricks which it called "miracles," from the boyars it created "saints," men of God—all for
the benefit of the authorities. The main task of all churches was
one and the same: to impress upon the poor serfs that there was
no happiness for them on earth; happiness was prepared for
them in heaven, and meanwhile back-breaking toil for some
other fellow was pleasing in the sight of God.

A peasant could not be admitted to the canon of saints, but
nobody stopped him from engaging in the sinful occupation of
farming with hired servants and of money-lending. All the
better for the big animal if the little animal is fat; he is all the
nicer to eat. The most shrewd and cunning among the working
people fought their way out of a dark, laborious, poverty-
stricken life and added to the number of those who sat on the
patient neck of the working people by sitting on it themselves.

In October 1917 a new history of humanity was begun in
our country. Every literate worker and peasant must learn it,
for the new history is being made in accordance with that

eternal truth, which draws onward the working people of the whole world, and has often fired them with the longing to realise it in practice, to build life on its foundation. This is the only truth with the power to improve all the conditions of life for the workers and peasants. The first man to prove beyond dispute that the old history of humanity was drawing to its end and that the time had come to create a new history—the history of the complete emancipation of the working people from the cruel yoke of the rich—this man was Karl Marx.

He and his successor, the genius Vladimir Lenin, firmly and permanently established the simple, clear truth: the life of the working people, the proletariat of town and village, cannot be changed for the better while the conditions exist which make it possible for one man to live on the labour of tens and hundreds of thousands of people. The penal conditions of labour and barbarous forms of social life which are built on greed, envy, incessant strife, and which senselessly exhaust the labour energy of the working people—these shameful conditions can be changed only by the working class. For this purpose the working class must take over political power; it must take over all the land and everything that it produces and yields when intelligent, systematic human labour is applied to it—everything useful to men that is hidden in the bowels of the earth; it must take over all the means of production: tools, machines, factories, ships, locomotives; it must take over everything that has been made and is being made by the labour of the workers, but which only serves to strengthen the meaningless and irresponsible rule of the capitalists.

We know that all socialists have accepted this as the truth, but the majority of them are settled in the opinion that such a drastic alteration can only be made in the main conditions of life of the working people by quietly and peacefully ironing out the contradictions between capital and labour, by gradual, slow "evolution." Hence it is clear that certain reactionary leaders of the Second International are not revolutionaries; they are indistinguishable from educated liberals who, while they agree "on principle" that the forms of social life must be changed, pursue in practice their own interests, the interests of people who wish to domineer over the lives of the working class. These socialists have betrayed the working class so many times that we could omit all mention of them, were it not for the fact that they are capable of further treasons and treachery.

In 1903 Lenin, a man of great and lucid intellect, a stalwart and strict revolutionary, flatly declared that the principal task of a true socialist was to develop the class instinct of the proletariat of town and village to a realisation of the necessity to organise an armed uprising against the landowners and manufacturers for the purpose of seizing political power.

His theory spread, it organised the class consciousness of the workers, created a party of sterling fighters and gave the proletariat victory over its enemies. In the country of the Union of Socialist Soviets there are no other masters than the workers and peasants, all its wealth belongs to them only.

The Soviet Union marks the beginning and the progressive advance in the construction of the first socialist state in the world. It is hard to extirpate the habits, prejudices, and superstitions inbred in people by ages, but this work of letting in the light and the air on the survivals of the old, dismal past is going ahead, and we can already say that there is no corner of the Soviet Union where the revolutionary spirit of the new history has not penetrated.

This revolutionary spirit will operate still more powerfully

The People Must Know

and effectively if we show the mass of workers and peasants a broad outline of the epic picture of the beginning of the new history. It began with the Civil War of 1918-21, an expression, vehement beyond all comparison, of the workers' and peasants' will, a historical picture of countless battles fought by a naked, hungry, almost unarmed proletariat against superbly equipped armies of officers and young bourgeois, commanded by generals who were masters of military science, helped by the capitalists of all Europe in their defence of the rule of the land-owners, manufacturers, bankers.

The history of the Civil War is the history of the triumph of a great truth embodied in the working class. This history should be familiar to every fighter on the front of cultural revolution, to every builder of the new world.

Work on such a book, a history of the Civil War, has been begun by Comrade Voroshilov and other military specialists with the collaboration, of course, of expert historians. This will be a book within the understanding of every reader, even one lacking in education. To make it easy to read, the best of our writers who were at the front during the Civil War, with rifle or pen, have been enlisted to handle the military material.*

This "History" is needed not only by the old fighters who are now hard at work building socialism, breaking down the resistance of ancient human inertia and people's mistrust of their own powers; it is needed not only to conjure up proud memories of their battles and victories. Our young generation needs it to learn the heroism of their fathers and to understand who were the men that fought for their cottage and cow, for the

---

* The first volume of this work—History of the Civil War in the U.S.S.R., edited by Stalin, Voroshilov, Gorky, and others—has been published (New York and London, 1937).—Trans.

victory of the working class, for socialism. It is needed by the proletariat of all countries, the millions for whom the days of great battles are now not far distant. This book must be a vivid chronicle of heroism and must inspire heroism.

At the same time it will be a real, veracious history of all the atrocities and havoc inflicted on our country by its former masters; it must show all the loathsome hatred felt by the beasts of prey who had had their claws cut and their teeth drawn. It will show how shamelessly the factory-owners and landowners destroyed the property of the people of their country. It will convince the good-natured and the soft-hearted that a capitalist is no longer a human being, but a creature in which an insane lust for profit has consumed every vestige of humanity. This "History" must be a record of all the blood shed by the capitalists for the sole purpose of maintaining their accustomed conditions of life, the comfortable, delightful, thoroughly corrupt life of two-legged beasts fattening themselves on other people's strength.

This will be the book of our socialist truth which has come to transform the old world and resurrect it, to a new life.

1930

ABOUT THE LITTLE OLD MEN

A QUESTIONNAIRE in the first issue of the magazine *Za Rubezhom* (Abroad) brought in a number of instructive and serious replies. One was from an "office employee, a non-party socialist, sixty and a half years of age."

He did not answer the questions in the questionnaire but, in a manner, went beyond them. First of all he pointed out that "the prospectus of the magazine had promised a truthful representation of life both at home and abroad." In this he was mistaken: there was not a word in the prospectus about any intention to represent "life at home" in the magazine; it was definitely stated in the prospectus that the magazine, as its name implies, would deal with life "Abroad." The error of the little old man may be explained by the weakness of his "non-party" eyesight—an incurable failing at his age.

But as we proceeded with his letter, this error quite unmistakably betrayed the "essence" of the little old man: he turned out to be a "humanist," nothing less! He reproached us for not saying anything in our magazine about the "Party purging," which the little old man calls "useless torture"—useless, because, as he says, "you can't find a man without moral defects."

Here it may be in place to remark that, in our conditions, the "humanitarian" view of the defective person has a rather serious practical significance: in the frank evidence given by the "wreckers" it has been repeatedly and convincingly brought

101

out that persons with "defects," "morally unstable," "disloyal," "useless for administrative work," with "anti-Soviet sentiments," and generally good-for-nothing, are useful for the job of state wrecking. It is exactly these people that are being thrown out of the Party in the purging which the little old man calls "useless," and "torture" to boot, apparently implying that there exists useful torture.

The humane little old man further makes the correct, albeit rather illiterate, statement that "Nowhere in the sublunar world does such deproletarianising (?) take place as the dekulakising that is going on in the U.S.S.R."

Yes, nowhere in the sublunar world—except the Soviet Union —has the working class as yet undertaken that necessary work which has been successfully begun in our country; but we are quite certain that *all the working people will inevitably follow our good example.* The meaning of this example is plain and clear: it is necessary to place the peasantry—the passive mass which is enslaved to the elemental forces of nature, which has for ages been exploited and has for ages bred in its midst the cruelest type of exploiters—in different conditions and to bring the toiling people up anew to become the masters of the earth instead of being its slaves. In other words: it is necessary to destroy the soil from which all the horrors of capitalism have developed. Hammelrat, a journalist on the staff of the German Catholic newspaper *New People*, recently wrote as follows about this gigantic work:

Here is concentrated energy, which demolishes the old and builds a new world. Seven million peasant households, twenty million people in the villages joined collective farms. The village poor are the mainstay of the whole collective farm movement. It is in this sphere—in the collective farm movement—that the figures of the Five-Year Plan have been greatly exceeded. . . . The Soviet press does not brag about the achievements, but urges the necessity of further achievements. When it writes of difficulties and failures, that should cause us no malicious glee but arouse our wonder, for this also is a manifestation of that same irrepressible energy which drives ever onward. This young insatiate energy is of decisive significance. Russia is becoming ever more independent of the rest of the world. This entails great sacrifices, but the sacrifices are made. The Five-Year Plan represents all the politics of the world for decades to come.

This is what an outsider says, a Catholic at that, a member of the church whose head proclaimed something like a crusade against the country and the people of the "non-party socialist." But the humane little old man is not interested in the process of the renascence of his people and in the great work of the "concentrated energy" of the working class in his fatherland. He informs us that "sick kulaks are wrapped three at a time in a piece of matting and taken away on a sleigh," apparently to hospital.

The writer has a certain idea of how mats are plaited, and he doubts whether there are mats in which you could wrap three persons apiece. Of course, it is a trifle—mats; but such trifles are always very characteristic of the "non-party" accusers and truth-lovers. While asserting his own truth, the truth-lover never has any qualms about telling a lie. The little old man concludes his letter with an appeal to "keep the promise to give a truthful and dispassionate representation of life."

Culture and the People

The editors can only reiterate what was said above: they set themselves the aim to represent life "Abroad." The aim of the magazine is to show the readers that life in Europe, America, and abroad generally, does not at all present a picture of nice prosperity, tender and reciprocal love between manufacturers and workers, landlords and peasants, clerks and bosses, of peaceful bliss and uninterrupted joy everywhere. The editors will readily bring to light the positive phenomena of life abroad in the spheres of science, technology, and art. The editors know well that so far they have not succeeded in doing their work with the necessary completeness and in perfect form.

But the editors do not promise the humane little old man that they will be dispassionate in representing the political situation and living conditions abroad. Dispassionateness means lack of passion. *We are passionate people, we hate passionately and we will be biassed—that's how you have to take us!* Nonparty, and for that matter Party, little old men of the ages between eighteen and seventy and over, can fully satisfy their thirst for the truth by reading our daily press, in which the truth of Soviet reality is represented passionately and mercilessly. We know that this passionate mercilessness in the exposure of the lazy, the saboteurs, the selfseeking, the quacks, fools, vulgarians, and other freaks is as a rejuvenating tonic to the little old men of all ages; we know that when they read of shortcomings and errors, of stupidity and baseness, they rejoice and dance on the brink of their graves. But we also know that our achievements are immeasurably greater than our shortcomings and that the fundamental, the greatest achievement is precisely the "concentrated energy" which is capable of working miracles.

As for his age, the little old man reduced it considerably; he

104

About the Little Old Men

is not sixty and a half years of age, but much older; in fact, he is monstrously old. He is not unique, and as a "type" belongs to that tribe of little old men of whom the Neapolitan Giordano Bruno wrote in 1583:

> What is the kind of peace and harmony that they offer the poor nations? Is not what they want, and what they dream of, that the whole world should consent to their malignant and most conceited ignorance and thus ease their sly conscience, while they themselves refuse to submit to the just doctrine?

For these and many other words in the same spirit, which Bruno wrote in his books, *The Banishment of the Triumphing Beast* and *On Heroic Enthusiasm,* the little old men kept Giordano Bruno in prison for seven years and then burnt him alive at the stake. And one of the little old men, Cardinal Gaspar Schopp, followed up Bruno's death with these words:

> Thus he was burned, thus he died a miserable death, and now, I think, he went to the other worlds which he invented for himself, to tell them how the Romans deal with the impious.

As you see, four hundred years before our time the little old men were just as monstrous and mischievous as they are to-day. And just as Cardinal Schopp rejoiced at the murder of Giordano Bruno, so our contemporary little old men rejoice over the murder of Jaures, Liebknecht, Rosa Luxembourg, Sacco and Vanzetti, and many other people of "heroic enthusiasm."

The monstrous longevity of the little old men is not only a sad fact but a hideous one as well, for it reveals how stagnant and dead is the life that has created the "little old men," and

105

how slowly the "psychology of the personality" changes. But at the same time this fact tells us that the personality is becoming ever more insignificant, and that it is "influencing the course of history as well" to an ever smaller degree. This process of the shrinking of the personality is excellently portrayed in European literature; in its main lines, this literature furnishes a vivid commentary on the history of the growth and development and the subsequent waning of the energy of the bourgeois class.

Literary artists have created a number of monumental figures of hypocrites, religious fiends, fanatics of "gain" and other pillars of the bourgeois world. In our times all these pillars have dwindled to the size of a Briand or a Chamberlain and similar masters at the art of repairing the chicken coop that is called the bourgeois state. Our literary scholars would be doing an important piece of work, and one that is pedagogically necessary for our youth, if they wrote a series of biographies of literary types. These would represent very interesting little histories of the deterioration of the personality. It would be very convenient to take, for instance, the type of Oliver Cromwell and trace in a series of similar figures the deterioration of this type to the dwarf-like figure of Alexander Kerensky.

The "great men" of the past are the direct ancestors of the little old men of our day, that is beyond dispute. But this does not increase the stature and importance of our little old man; it only shows to what microscopic proportions the "great ones" have shrunk.

Our little old man is an inconsequential person, but he is also typical. His principal characteristic is: a tender love of himself, and love for the "eternal truths" which he found in various evangels, and for the "cursed questions" for which there is no solution in words. Here, for instance, is what a little old man of twenty-six years writes: "What am I, sitting here, whose fate, like that of everything living, is to be dead?"

This is the form in which the beautiful phrase of Ecclesiastes is cast to-day! And in this same way everything is more or less successfully distorted by the idlers and word-adulterers to whom, in the long run, the most interesting thing in the world is the corn on their foot. One of them says so in so many words: "We are building universities and institutes, but we have not learned to cure a plain corn." Another writes in a divinely-grand manner: "Reality parted ways with me, she did not understand me." Just imagine, how cruelly this capricious reality behaved! *It is the personality of the philistine that is deteriorating, it is his thought, crammed with rubbish and poisoned by his vile mode of life, that is deteriorating.* Dexterous grabber, money-lender, slave to gain and, in the past, builder of the iron cage of the state, the philistine has become a pigmy.

But although he is puny, he is harmful none the less, as dust is harmful, as the miasma of marshes and the gases of decaying organic matter are harmful. There are many poisonous admixtures in the air which we breathe. They are very injurious and must be fought "with might and main." The history of culture must be written as the history of the deterioration of the personality, as the description of the road it travelled to its death, and as the history of the rise of the new personality which is being shaped in the fire of the "concentrated energy" of the builders of the new world.

930

REPLY TO AN INTELLECTUAL

YOU write: "Many intellectuals in Western Europe are beginning to feel that they are people without a fatherland, and our thoughts are now turning more and more toward life in Russia. At the same time what is actually going on in the Soviet Union is still hazy in our minds."

The Soviet Union is the scene of a struggle between the rationally organised will of the working masses and the forces of spontaneity in both nature and man. This "spontaneity" in man is nothing more nor less than the instinctive anarchy of the individual which has become ingrained in the course of ages through his oppression by the class state.

This struggle is the sum and substance of reality in the Soviet Union. Any one who sincerely desires to understand the profound meaning of the revolutionary cultural changes which have overtaken old Russia will grasp their import only by regarding this process as a struggle for culture and for the creative potentialities of culture.

You Westerners have adopted an attitude toward the people of the Soviet Union which I can hardly consider worthy of persons who consider themselves apostles of a culture which they deem indispensable for the whole world. It is the attitude of a tradesman to his customer, of a creditor to his debtor. You remember that tsarist Russia borrowed money from you and learned from you how to think; but you forget that these loans yielded your industrialists and merchants uncommonly luscious profits, and that Russian science of the nineteenth and twentieth centuries contributed much to the general stream of European scientific research. To-day, when it is so distressingly clear that your creative power in the sphere of art is on the decline, you are living on the forces, the ideas and forms of Russian art. You cannot gainsay the fact that Russian music and literature, not to be outdone by Russian science, long ago won an honoured place in the body of world culture.

It would seem that a people whose spiritual creative capacity has risen in the course of one century to heights comparable to those achieved by the rest of Europe in the course of many centuries, a people which has but now gained freedom in the use of its creative powers, deserves closer study and attention than has hitherto been accorded it by the intellectuals of Europe.

Is it not time that you definitely made up your minds to ask yourselves this question: Just what are the differences between the objectives of the bourgeoisie of Europe and of the peoples of the Soviet Union? It is sufficiently clear by now that the political leaders of Europe do not serve "the nation as a whole," but serve mutually hostile groups of capitalists. This mutual hostility among the leaders of big business, who were devoid of any sense of responsibility to their respective "nations," resulted in a series of crimes against humanity similar to the world holocaust of 1914-18. It intensified mutual distrust among nations, turned Europe into a row of armed camps and now squanders an enormous amount of the people's labour, gold, and iron in the manufacture of ammunition with which to perpetrate new massacres. Owing to this antagonism between the capitalists, the world economic crisis, which drains the physical resources of the "nation" and stunts the growth of its intellectual forces, has been sharply aggravated. This enmity among robbers and hucksters is preparing the way for a new world carnage.

Ask yourselves: What purpose is served by all this? And, generally speaking, if you sincerely want to be relieved of your burden of doubt and your negative attitude toward life, ponder over this simplest of questions regarding the existing social order. Without allowing yourselves to be carried away by words, give serious thought to the general aims of capitalist existence—or, to be more exact, to the criminal character of its existence.

You intellectuals are said to "cherish culture, whose universal significance is indisputable." Is that really so? Under your very noses capitalism is day by day steadily destroying this precious culture in Europe, and by its inhuman and cynical policies in the colonies is most certainly creating a host of enemies of European culture. If this rapacious "culture" of yours is producing a few thousand similarly minded robbers on the black and yellow continents, do not forget that some hundreds of millions still remain within the fold of the plundered and poverty-stricken. Hindus, Chinese, and Annamites bow their heads before your cannon, but that does not in the least mean that they venerate European culture. And they are beginning to realise that in the Soviet Union a different sort of culture is springing up, different in form and in significance.

"Heathens and savages dwell in the East," you declare; and in proof of this assertion you harp on the position of women in the East. Let us go into this question of savages.

In European music-halls scores and hundreds of women appear nude on the stage. Does it not strike you that such a public exhibition of the naked female ought to call forth some protest from the mothers, wives, and sisters of the European intellectuals? I am discussing the significance of this cynical pastime not from the "moral" point of view but with an eye to biology and social hygiene. To me this vile and vulgar pastime is indisputable proof of the savagery and of the deep-going decadence of the European bourgeoisie. I am convinced that the evident and rapid growth of homosexuality and Lesbianism, which find their economic explanation in the high cost of family life, is accelerated by this disgusting public spectacle of burlesque women.

There is far too much evidence of savagery in bourgeois Europe, and it ill befits you to speak of the barbarism of the East. The peasantry of the nations which have entered the Soviet Union is fast learning the value of genuine culture and the importance of the part woman plays in life. The truth of this is fully appreciated by the workers and peasants in those provinces of China in which Soviets have already been established. The Hindus, too, will learn to understand. All the toiling masses of our planet must sooner or later discover the road to freedom. It is precisely for this freedom that they are struggling all over the world.

In the capitalist world the struggle for oil, for iron, and for the arming of millions in preparation for a new slaughter, rages with increasing fury. It is a struggle conducted by a minority for the right to the political and economic oppression of the majority. This brazen, cynical, criminal struggle, organised by a small group of people goaded to savagery by the senseless thirst for money, is blessed by the Christian church, which is the most deceitful and the most criminal church in the world. This struggle has completely exterminated "humanitarianism," which was so dear to the hearts of the European intellectuals and of which they were so proud.

Culture and the People

Never before had the intellectuals so clearly displayed their helplessness and their shameless indifference to life as they have in the twentieth century, so full of the tragedies created by the cynicism of the ruling classes. In the sphere of politics, the sentiments and ideology of the intellectuals are under the thumb of adventurers humbly serving the will of capitalist groups, who trade in everything that is marketable and, in the end, always bargain away the energy of the people. By this word "people," I mean not only the workers and peasants, but also petty officials and the army of "employees" of capitalism, and the intellectuals as a whole—still a bright patch among the filthy tatters of bourgeois society.

Carried away by verbose investigations into that which is "common to all humanity," the polygot intellectuals survey one another from behind the wall of their respective national and class prejudices.

The failings and vices of their neighbours are, therefore, of more interest to them than their virtues. They have fought one another so often that they no longer remember who has the greatest number of victories or defeats to his credit, and deserves to be treated with corresponding respect. Capitalism has inspired them with a sceptical distrust of one another and plays cleverly on this feeling.

They did not understand the historic importance of the October Revolution and they had neither the strength nor the desire to protest against the bloody and predatory capitalist intervention of 1918-21. They protest when a monarchist professor or plotter is arrested in the Soviet Union, but they remain indifferent when their capitalists violate the peoples of Indo-China, India, and Africa. When, in the Soviet Union, a half-hundred of the most infamous criminals are shot, the foreign

112

intellectuals fill the air with their clamorous outcries against savagery; but when, in India or Annam, thousands of totally innocent people are wiped out by cannon and machine-guns, these humane intellectuals are modestly silent. They are still unable to draw conclusions from the results of years of toil and of inestimable energy spent in the Soviet Union. The politicians in Parliament and in the press fill their ears with tales of how the work of the Soviets is directed exclusively to the destruction of the "old world," and they do not fail to believe that this is so.

But in the Soviet Union the working masses are rapidly assimilating all that is best and most precious in the cultural heritage of mankind. This process of assimilation is accompanied by a process of development of this heritage. Naturally, we are destroying the old world, for we must release man from the multiplicity of shackles which have impeded his intellectual growth and free his mind from superstition and all the time-worn concepts of class, nationality, and church.

The fundamental aim of the cultural process in the Soviet Union is the unification of all the peoples of the world into one indivisible whole. This work is dictated by the entire course of the history of mankind; it is the beginning not merely of a national, but of a world renaissance. Individuals like Campanella, Thomas More, Saint-Simon, Fourier, and others dreamt of this at a time when the industrial technique necessary for the realisation of this dream was as yet non-existent. Now all requisite conditions exist. The dream of the utopians has found a firm foundation in science, and the work of realising this dream is being carried on by millions. In another generation there will be nearly two hundred million workers engaged in this work in the Soviet Union alone.

113

Culture and the People

When people do not want to understand or have not the strength to understand, they take refuge in blind belief.

Class instinct, the psychology of the petty proprietor and the philosophy of those who blindly support class society, force these intellectuals to believe that individual expression is smothered and suppressed in the Soviet Union, that the industrialization of the country is proceeding by means of the same kind of forced labour that built the Egyptian pyramids. This is not an ordinary lie, but the kind of obvious lie which deceives only those who are absolutely impotent and with no sense of personal responsibility, people who are living in a state of complete decadence and whose intellectual energy and critical thought have been completely exhausted.

The rapidity with which great numbers of talented people are emerging in all walks of life—in art, science, and technology—conclusively disproves this myth of the suppression of individuality in the U.S.S.R. It could not be otherwise in a land where the entire population is drawn into the cultural process.

Out of twenty-five million "private owners," semi-literate and totally illiterate peasants oppressed by the autocracy of the Romanovs and the landed bourgeoisie, twelve million have already come to appreciate the reasonableness and advantages of collective farming. This new form of labour frees the peasant from his instincts for conservatism and anarchism as well as from the animal-like mentality common to petty proprietorship. It offers him considerable leisure, which he uses to liquidate his own illiteracy. To-day, in 1931, there are fifty million adults and children attending schools; and the literature planned and issued during this year comes to eight hundred million books, or about fifty billion printed pages. Popular demand has al-

114

ready reached eighty billion printed pages, but the factories cannot supply that amount of paper.

The thirst for knowledge is growing. Since the establishment of the Soviet Union dozens of scientific research institutes, new universities, and polytechnic schools have been founded. All of them are filled to overflowing with throngs of young students, while the masses of the workers and peasants are constantly developing thousands of new leaders of culture.

Has it ever been, and can it ever be, the aim of a bourgeois state to draw all the millions of its working people into cultural activities? History answers this simple question negatively. Capitalism promotes the mental development of the workers only in so far as is necessary and profitable for industry and trade. Capitalism needs human beings only as a more or less inexpensive source of power for the defence of the existing order.

Capitalism has not reached and never can reach the simple realisation that the aim and significance of genuine culture is the development and accumulation of intellectual energy. In order that this energy may develop uninterruptedly and thereby assist humanity the sooner to utilise all the forces and gifts of nature, it is essential to liberate the maximum amount of physical energy from these senseless and anarchic drudgeries which serve the greedy interests of the capitalists, plunderers and parasites of toiling humanity. The conception of humanity as a storage plant filled with an enormous supply of intellectual energy is absolutely foreign to the ideologists of capitalism. In spite of all their shrewdness in wielding the pen and their eloquence in the spoken word, the ideology of those who defend the rule of the minority over the majority is essentially bestial.

Culture and the People

Class states are built after the fashion of zoological gardens where all the animals are imprisoned in iron cages. In class states these cages, constructed with varying degrees of skill, serve to prolong those ideas which divide humanity and prevent the development of an awareness in man of his own interests as well as the birth of a genuine culture embracing all humanity.

Is it necessary for me to deny that the individual in the Soviet Union is restricted? Of course not, and I do not deny it. In the Soviet Union the will of the individual is restricted when it runs counter to the will of the masses, who are aware of their right to build new forms of life; who have set themselves a task beyond the power of any single individual even if he be gifted with the genius of a superman. The front ranks of the workers and peasants in the Soviet Union are advancing towards their own lofty ideal, heroically overcoming a multitude of obstacles and difficulties in the way.

The individual defends his sham freedom and apparent independence inside his cage. The cages in which the writers, journalists, philosophers, government officials, and all the other well-greased cogs of the capitalist machine are confined are naturally more comfortable than the peasant's cage. The peasant's smoky and filthy hut and his "private patch of ground" keep him alert, on the watch against the capricious destructiveness of nature's elemental forces, and against the attacks of the capitalist state which flays him alive. The farmers of Calabria, Bavaria, Hungary, and Great Britain, of Africa and America, do not differ greatly from one another psychologically, except in the use of language. Throughout the entire globe the peasant lives in the same more or less isolated manner and is infected with a primitive individualism. In the Soviet

116

Union the peasant by going over to collective farming is gradually weaning himself away from this psychology of the slave of the soil, the attitude of the eternal prisoner of an impoverished proprietorship.

Individualism is the result of external pressure brought to bear on man by class society. Individualism is a sterile attempt by the individual to defend himself against violence. But self-defence is self-limitation, since in a state of self-defence the process of intellectual growth is retarded. Such a state is harmful alike to society and to the individual. "Nations" spend billions on armaments against their neighbours; the individual expends most of his energy defending himself against the violence to which he is subjected by class society. "Life is a struggle?" Yes, but life ought to be a struggle of man against the elemental forces of nature, with the object of subduing and directing them. Class society has debased this lofty struggle into an abject fight to master the physical energy of man and to enslave him.

The individualism of the intellectual of the nineteenth and twentieth centuries differs from that of the peasant in form of expression only. It is more flowery, more polished, but just as primitive and blind. The intellectual finds himself between the upper mill-stone of the people and the nether mill-stone of the state. As a rule, the conditions of his existence are harsh and full of drama, since his surroundings are generally hostile. That is why his imprisoned thoughts so often cause him to place the burden of his own conditions of life on the whole world, and these subjective conceptions give rise to philosophical pessimism, scepticism, and other deformities of thought. It is well known that the birthplace of pessimism is the East, particularly India, where the caste system has been carried to the height of fanaticism.

Class society cramps the growth of the individual. That is why the individual seeks a place and peace outside and beyond reality; for example, in God. The toiling masses seeking an explanation for the elemental forces of nature, benevolent and malevolent, have cleverly incarnated these phenomena in a being having human characteristics but mightier than man himself. The people endowed their gods with all the virtues and vices which they themselves possessed. The Olympian gods are exaggerated human beings; Vulcan and Thor are blacksmiths, such as you might find in any village, but infinitely more powerful, if not more skilful.

The religious images created by people of toil are simply artistic creations, devoid of mysticism; they are essentially realistic and true to reality. They clearly reveal the influence of the daily toil of their creators; in fact this art aims at stimulating their activity. The consciousness that the world of reality is the creation not of the gods, but of their own productive energy, is also apparent in the poetry of the people. The masses are pagans. Even fifteen hundred years after Christianity became the state religion, the peasantry still envisaged the gods as the gods of old: Christ, the Madonna, and the saints stalk the earth and share in the day's toil of the people just as the gods of the ancient Greeks and Scandinavians.

Individualism sprang from the soil of "private ownership." Generations upon generations of men were engaged in building up the collective, and always the individual, for one reason or another, has stood apart, breaking away from the collective and at the same time from reality where the new is ever in the making. He has been creating his own unique, mystical, and incomprehensible god, set up for the sole purpose of justifying the right of the individual to independence and power. Here mysticism becomes indispensable, because the right of the individual to absolute rule, to "autocracy," cannot be explained by reason. Individualism endowed its god with the qualities of omnipotence, infinite wisdom, and absolute intelligence—with qualities which man would like to possess, but which develop only through the reality created by collective labour. This reality always lags behind the human mind, for the mind which creates it is slowly but constantly perfecting itself. If this were not so, reality would, of course, make people contented, and the state of contentment is a passive one. Reality is created by the inexhaustible and intelligent will of man, and its development will never be arrested.

The mystic god of the individualist has always remained and always will remain immovable, inactive, creatively dead. It cannot be otherwise, for this god reflects the inherent weakness of the creative forces of individualism. The history of the individualist's sterile and hair-splitting distinctions, drawn in his religious and metaphysical speculations, are well known to every educated person. In our own time the futility of these speculative niceties as well as the complete bankruptcy of the philosophy of individualism has been clearly and irrefutably exposed. But the individualist still continues his barren quest for the answer to the "riddle of life." He seeks it not in the reality of labour, which is developing in every direction at a revolutionary pace, but in the depths of his own ego. He continues to cling to his miserable little "private estate" and has no desire to enrich life. He is busy cogitating measures of self-defence; he does not live, he hides; in his "contemplative activity" he recalls the biblical hero, Onan.

119

Culture and the People

Humbly submitting to the exigencies of the capitalist state, the intellectuals of Europe and America—the writers, the publicists, the economists, the ex-Socialists who have of late blossomed forth as adventurers and as dreamers of the type of Gandhi—consciously or unconsciously defend bourgeois class society, a society which obstinately impedes the process of development of human culture. In this process the will of the working masses, directed toward the creation of a new reality, plays the most important *rôle*. The intellectuals think they are defending "democracy," although this democracy of theirs has already proved and continues to prove its impotence. They defend "personal freedom," although this freedom is imprisoned in a cage of ideas which imposes sharp limitations upon individual growth. They defend "the freedom of the press," although the press is at the beck and call of the capitalists and can serve only their anarchic, human, and criminal interests. The intellectual works for his own enemy; for the master has always been the enemy of the worker. The idea of "class collaboration" is just as naïve and absurd as friendship between wolves and lambs.

The intellectuals of Europe and America are working for their enemies, as is shown in a particularly glaring and shameless way by their attitude towards the revolutionary cultural process which has started among the masses of workers and peasants in the Soviet Union. This process is developing in an atmosphere of frenzied hostility on the part of the European bourgeoisie, and under the threat of a vicious attack on the Soviet Union. The influence of these two factors serves to explain almost completely these negative phases which the enemies of the workers and peasants of the Soviet Union are so anxious to emphasise.

Reply to an Intellectual

These negative aspects of Soviet life appeal in particular to those malicious Russian émigrés who dabble in politics and who serve the European bourgeois press as sources of "information" about the Soviet Union.

Who are these émigrés? The majority of them are political failures, ambitious small-fry with "great hopes." Some of them would like to be Briands and Churchills; many of them would like to be Fords; it is characteristic of all of them that they have tried to attain executive posts by foul means. For some time past I have been well aware of their moral and intellectual poverty. This they showed as far back as 1905-07, during and after the first revolution, and, later when they daily demonstrated their impotence in the Duma. Again, during 1914-17, they showed it with utmost clearness when they pretended to "fight against autocracy," but were in reality champions of Pan-Russian chauvinism. They enjoyed some measure of popularity by organising the political consciousness of the petty and big bourgeoisie. Broadly speaking, they are the ideologists of the philistine. There is a saying: "If you can't get lobster, crab will have to do." The part they played in Russian life was that of crabs, always moving backwards. This, generally, is the role of the majority of intellectuals during revolutionary periods.

But their ignominious *rôle* is not confined to constant political "changes of front" and to forgetting the oath which Hannibal vowed. In 1917, they joined the remnant of the tsar's generals, who had despised them and dubbed them renegades and "enemies of the tsar." Together with these scoundrelly bedfellows these intellectuals entered the services of the Russian oil, textile, and coal magnates and big landowners.

In Russian history they are known as traitors to their own

121

people. During a period of four years they betrayed and sold their people to your capitalists, Mr. European Intellectual. They helped Denikin, Kolchak, Wrangel, Yudenich, and other professional murderers to destroy the national economy of their country, already ravaged by a slaughter which shamed all Europe. With the help of these contemptible vermin, the generals of the European capitalists and of the former tsar slaughtered hundreds of thousands of the workers and peasants of the Soviet Union. They razed hundreds of villages and Cossack hamlets, destroyed railways, blew up bridges, and devastated everything in their path, bringing their country to the brink of destruction in order to assure delivery into the hands of the European capitalists. If you were to ask them why they butchered their own people and destroyed their homes, they would answer quite unabashed: "For the sake of the people" —and not breathe a word about how that same "people" flung them unceremoniously out of their country.

After 1926 they were involved in the organisation of numerous plots against the workers' and peasants' state. Needless to say, they deny participation in these crimes, although the conspirators—their friends—confessed that they furnished the press with notoriously false information about the activities of the Soviets. The conspirators, in their turn, were guided by the press of these traitors to their country.

Your humanitarianism, gentlemen of Europe, was roused to indignation by the well-merited sentence passed upon the forty-eight sadists who deliberately set out to starve the country.* How strange that you are not moved to protest against the almost daily murder of perfectly innocent workers by the

* A group of officials in the food industry and cold storage plants who carried on wrecking activities.—*Trans.*

police in the streets of your cities? Forty-eight degenerates are far more disgusting than that Dusseldorf sadist, Kurten, who was sentenced to death nine times. I do not know the motives which prompted the Soviet government not to turn these conspirators over to the regular courts, but I think I can guess the reason. There are crimes whose vileness is peculiarly pleasant to the enemies of the Soviets, and to instruct an enemy in such depravity, would be asking rather too much. But I will say this: if I were a German citizen I would have protested against the public trial of Kurten. Class society has already made far too many sadists; and I see no need or justification for advertising sadism and thus raising the technical skill of criminals.

May I ask why the European intellectuals defend "personal liberty" when the person in question is, for example, Professor S. F. Platonov, a monarchist, yet remain indifferent when the person in question is a Communist?

If you want to know the exact degree of savagery of which Russian émigrés are capable, read the appeal for contributions to the fund raised for the struggle against the people of the Soviet Union, published in the Paris organ of the monarchist émigrés, *Vozrozhdyeniye* (Regeneration).

At the head of this base and vulgar venture is "His Beneficence, the Metropolitan Anthony, president of the Synod of Archbishops of the Orthodox Church Abroad." Here are the actual words of this fanatic:

> By the authority given to me by God, I bless every weapon used against the red Satanical power which has raised its head, and I absolve from sin all those in the ranks of the insurgent bands and those who, as individual

avengers of their nation, will give their lives for Russia
and for Jesus. First and above all, I bless every weapon
and every militant deed of the Universal Brotherhood of
the Truth of Russia, which has fought unflinchingly for
many years, in word and deed, against the red Satan in
the name of God and Russia. God's mercy will rest upon
all you who enter their fraternal ranks, for brotherhood
will surely rescue and deliver you.

Anthony, Metropolitan.

It is thus perfectly clear that the Metropolitan, a leader of
the Christian church, gives his blessing to all those who violate the will of the people of the Soviet Union and commit acts
of terrorism against them.

Do you not think that such appeals, such benedictions be-
stowed upon murder by a priest evidently enraged to the point
of idiocy, are somewhat out of place in the capital of a "civilised" state? Do you not think that you should tell his
Beneficence to hold his tongue? Does it not strike you that this
frenzied outburst of a Russian priest is a sign not only of the
unmitigated barbarity of the Russian émigrés, but also of the
utterly shameful indifference of European intellectuals to questions of social morality and social hygiene? And you dare
speak of the "savagery of the East"!

You believe the evidence of the Russian émigrés. Very well.
That is your "own affair"; but I doubt whether you have the
right to believe as you do. I doubt it because you are plainly
not interested in the evidence of the opposite side—the side
of the workers' and peasants' state. The Soviet press does not
conceal the bad sides of life in the Soviet Union. On the contrary, it uncovers every possible shortcoming, for it is based

on the principle of the severest self-criticism, and there are no skeletons to be hidden away in the cupboard.

The Soviet press must act as a news channel and organ of information for millions of people, most of whom are not yet altogether literate—through no fault of their own, you can be assured. But an honourable person will always bear in mind that a semi-literate person is quite apt to make mistakes. It should also be noted that most of the lies and calumnies on which the émigré press battens and consoles itself, seek some semblance of justification in points raised by Soviet self-criticism.

Personally, I protested in the press and at meetings in Moscow and Leningrad against this overdoing of self-criticism. I know with what voluptuous delight the émigrés pounce upon news items which might in any way feed their morbid hatred of the workers and peasants of the Soviet Union.

Not long ago an article of mine appeared in the Soviet press dealing with a book by Brehm, the Russian translation of which had been butchered by a careless old hack of rather meagre learning. Immediately the editor of the émigré newspaper *Ruhl,** Josef Hassen, a very stupid and ludicrously ill-tempered old fogy, published an editorial in which he announced with clownish glee that "even Gorky criticises the Soviet government!" He knows perfectly well that I have never hesitated to speak my mind quite openly about people who turn out careless, unconscientious, or bad work. But like all the other émigré "politicians," he simply cannot help lying.

There is a special kind of "truth" which serves as spiritual food for misanthropes only, for sceptics whose scepticism is founded on ignorance, and for indifferent people who seek jus-

---

* The Berlin organ of a group of counter-revolutionary émigrés.—*Trans.*

tification for their indifference. This is a putrid, moribund "truth;" this offal is fit only for pigs. This kind of truth is being cut out, root and branch, by the work of the advance guard of the builders of a new culture in the Soviet Union. I realise full well how this "truth" interferes with the work of honest folk; but I am opposed to the idea of giving sustenance and consolation to people who have justly been humiliated by the verdict of history.

You ask: "Are there discontented elements among the workers and peasants, and what causes their discontent?" To be sure, there is no distinct class of discontented people; but it would be miraculous indeed, after only thirteen years of labour under the dictatorship of the proletariat, if one hundred and sixty million people enjoyed absolute satisfaction of all their wants and desires. Such discontent as exists is readily explained by the simple fact that the apparatus of production and distribution cannot catch up with the rapidly growing cultural needs of the working masses in so short a space of time as thirteen years. There is a shortage of many things and quite a few people grumble and complain.

These complaints might be dismissed as ridiculous for they are premature and ill-considered; but I will not call them ridiculous because they are expressed with the firm and unmistakable conviction that the Soviet power is capable of satisfying all the needs of the country. Of course, those formerly well-to-do peasants who hoped that the revolution would enable them to become large-scale farmers and big landowners and would deliver the poor peasantry into their hands, are dissatisfied and even actively opposed to the work of the Soviet government. It stands to reason that this section of the peasantry would be antagonistic to collectivisation and would champion private property, hired labour, and all the other bourgeois paraphernalia which would lead inevitably to a rebirth of capitalist forms of life. But the game played by this section of the peasantry has already been lost, its resistance to collective farming is hopeless and only continues through sheer inertia.

In the more active ranks of the workers and peasants, no complaints are heard. They work. They know well enough that they are the government, that all their needs and desires can be satisfied only by dint of their own efforts. It is this realisation of their own abundant strength and their absolute power that has called forth such popular manifestations as socialist competition, shock brigades, and other unmistakable signs of the creative activity and heroism of labour. It was due to the consciousness of all this that a whole series of enterprises completed their Five-Year Plan in two and a half years.

The workers understand the thing that it is essential for them to understand: that power is in their own hands. In bourgeois states, laws are concocted and handed down from above; they are made for the purpose of strengthening the power of the ruling class. Legislation in the Soviet Union originates with the lowest bodies, in the village Soviets and in factory committees. If you watch the course of any such legislation, you will readily be convinced that these measures do not merely meet an immediate need of the working masses, but are convincing proof of the cultural growth of these masses.

The working and peasant masses of the Soviet Union are beginning to understand that the process of their material advancement and cultural development is being tampered with artificially by hostile European and American capitalists. Understanding this, of course, greatly increases their political self-consciousness and their own strength.

If the intellectuals of Europe and America, instead of listening to scandal-mongers, instead of trusting traitors, gave serious and honest thought to the historical significance of the process which is developing in the Soviet Union, they would understand that the object of this whole process is the assimilation of the invaluable treasures of universal culture by a nation of one hundred and sixty million people. They would understand that this nation labours not only for itself but for all humanity, at the same time revealing to mankind what miracles may be accomplished by the intelligently organised will of the masses.

Finally, I must categorically ask this question: Do the intellectuals of Europe and America want a new world massacre which will still further decrease their ranks and augment both their impotence and savagery? The worker and peasant masses of the Soviet Union do not want a war. They want to create a state where all will be equal. But in the event of an attack they will rise to a man to defend themselves as one indivisible whole, and they will be victorious because history is working for them.

1931

A LETTER TO THE WORKERS
OF MAGNITOSTROI

Dear Comrades,

Thanks for your invitation to visit your industrial strong-holds. I should like very much to watch you creating the gigantic factories, talk with you, learn from you, but I have no time for the journey. I am busy on a work which, some day, I hope, you will appreciate as being of value to you. You know that every one must do his job to the best of his ability and with all his energy. The best among you know this particularly well, and their labour heroism serves as an example for all the working people of the Soviet Union, and serves as an example for me as well. Time is valuable to us. We must not waste a single minute. The problems we must solve are enormous. Never before has any one, any nation in the world, set itself such difficult aims and tasks as the working class of the Union of Soviet Socialist Republics has set itself and is achieving.

We must, in the shortest possible time, destroy the whole past and create completely new conditions of life, conditions which exist nowhere else. We must equip our peasantry, who number many millions, with machines; must ease their laborious toil, make the land more fertile, teach them to fight drought and other caprices of nature which destroy the crops. We must lay thousands of miles of good roads, wipe out the crowded dirty villages, build good cities, with schools, thea-

129

tres, public bathhouses, hospitals, clubs, bakeries, and laundries for the workers of the field; in short, we must enrich them with all that the city abounds in, and which long since distinguished the customs, habits, peculiar social life, and "mentality" of the people of the city from those of the people of the village. We must eradicate this pernicious distinction which has been forced upon us by past history. We must train ourselves to become qualitatively different: we must eradicate from our nature all the accursed "past," we must become imbued with greater confidence in the all-conquering power of intelligent labour and technique.

We must become unselfish, learn to think about all things socialistically. We must subordinate our petty, personal interests to great problems, the solution of which demands that we work to construct the first state in the world in which there will be no class distinctions, in which there will be neither rich nor poor, neither masters nor servants; in which the main cause of all poverty and suffering will disappear, as will also the striving to acquire private property, which is the basis of envy, greed, and stupidity. We are building a state in which every one will work according to his ability and receive according to his needs, in which every one will feel that he is master of all the wealth of his country, in which the gates of knowledge will be wide open for every one. We want to create a new humanity, and we have already begun to create it.

From a number of letters I have received I gather that not every one, by far, understands that selfishness is the father of baseness, and that not every one has grown tired of living that mean, stupid life which our grandfathers and great-grandfathers lived. In your midst, comrades, there are many who have been poisoned by the past. These come from the coun-

A Letter to Workers

tryside in increasing numbers. But at heart you are sound, and in your environment even the most inveterate individualist is transformed. You gradually imbue them with your labour energy, and it is no longer true to use the Russian proverb that, "Only the grave can cure the hunchback." The socialist heroism of the working class is curing them.

However, you must tirelessly impress upon the people of the old world that their grandfathers and great-grandfathers had no other path to tread except the bad and narrow path to the rich. This path could be travelled only on the backs of the poor, on the backs of our class brothers—that is how our grandfathers and great-grandfathers acquired great wealth, but lost their conscience, and increased the oppressive burden of the rich upon the poor. Great wealth grows like mould. The richer a person becomes the less he loves mankind, and the more greedily does he squeeze from the poor roubles mingled with flesh and blood.

We now see what the capitalists of Europe and America have come to: they have grown tremendously, fantastically rich, but they have heaped up thirty-five million unemployed; thousands of rich are wallowing in wealth, while millions of poor are dying of starvation. Suppose every one of the thirty-five million unemployed was able to spend at least a rouble a day—how much profit would fall into the pockets of the capitalists?

There are lots of things to sell but no one to buy. The capitalists do not want to sell cheaply. They prefer to destroy the surplus goods in order to keep prices up. This sounds infamous, but it is true. On August 14, the European newspapers carried the following cable from America:

Culture and the People

New York, August 12. The Federal Farm Board has notified the governors of 14 cotton growing states of its recommendation to destroy one-third of the 1931 cotton crop in order to raise cotton prices.

This cable is not an invention. American papers confirm it. The *Washington Post* expressed the opinion that the destruction of valuable products at a time when millions are starving was a "humiliating commentary on the mental state of America."

... What has happened to the productive forces of America, that wheat and cotton have to be burned or allowed to rot in the fields while millions of citizens are in need of both?

It has often been said that the criminal, inhuman activity of the capitalists can only be explained by the fact that they are insane, only by the fact that their passion for gain, for accumulating wealth, has driven them mad. This is said metaphorically in order to "heighten the effect," in order to emphasise more clearly the brazenness of the plunderers of the world. But reality justifies even these words. *Vozvozhdenie* (*Renaissance*), a paper published by the monarchist émigrés in Paris, informs us that:

John O'Bannon, a millionaire, has appealed to the court in New York to nullify the demand of the doctors to have him committed to a lunatic asylum. The millionaire told the judge the story of his life. He started by inventing some substitute for leather, organized a company and acquired a fortune of 15 million dollars. Suffering from nerves, he went to a physician who declared him insane and had him committed to a lunatic asylum. In a very short time, even while in the asylum, he added two million dollars to his fortune. He even displayed business ability in the hospital and suggested improvements to its director to make it pay better. Specialists were summoned to the court to give evidence, but they testified this prominent business man was nonetheless insane, and so he was again sent to the mental hospital.

The only conclusion one can make from this fact is that the methods employed by capitalists to rob workers are so simple that even an obviously insane person can easily amass millions. The capitalist system is more and more openly and cynically becoming a system of banditism, while social life has reached a state of unconcealed anarchy. This is openly admitted in the American press. For example, the papers recently published the following news-item from America:

Chicago is not the only city that deserves the name of "home of the gangsters"; the same may be said of almost any city in the United States of any size.

And the Wickersham Commission, appointed by President Hoover to investigate the state of prisons and the detection of crime, wrote quite frankly in its report:

In nearly every large city there is an alliance between the police and the underworld. . . . In cities where the chief of police must be blindly obedient to orders from the Mayor, and where that dignitary is the political creature of killers and crooks of every conceivable character, administration of police affairs must of necessity sink to the level of those elements who hold controlling influence.

Culture and the People

To what this leads everybody can see by what is taking place in Chicago, New York, and San Francisco, where gangsters rob and kill in broad daylight.

Recently, during a shooting affray between gangsters in the streets of Chicago, four children were killed. Generally speaking, in the little war between the police and between gangsters, not much consideration is given to passersby, while murder of innocent citizens by the police is generally regarded as "accidental manslaughter" and is not punishable.

The capitalist world is dying, decaying. It has no strength to recuperate, it has evidently wasted its forces completely. This world continues to exist mechanically, by inertia, supported only by the brute force of the police. The army is not a very reliable force because the majority of the soldiers are proletarians, and although their heads are stuffed with the rubbish of petty-bourgeois prejudices, their political, class, revolutionary consciousness cannot but grow under present conditions. A world social revolution is not a fantasy but an inevitable and maturing event. In Europe, in addition to the police and the army, the capitalists are supported by the "leaders" of Social-Democracy and by a section of the workers fooled by the "leaders" who strive for power and fame. The conduct of these leaders is becoming increasingly disgraceful. Here is an example; Lord Lothian, who came here with Bernard Shaw, said, after he returned to England:

> The Russian Revolution contains ideas which will have tremendous influence on the subsequent development of mankind. We are faced with the problem of how to adapt them here [i.e., in England].

The head of the Social-Democrats, Vandervelde, in an article

134

attacking Lord Lothian, declared that "if the privileged world begins to reason like Lothian, then the time for the overthrow of capitalism will come very quickly." There is no ring of joy in the words of this "leader" of the working class; on the contrary, they plainly express the grief of an old lackey who is afraid that to-morrow his master will be driven out.

"Socialists" who tell the capitalists, "You are not holding to your class position firmly enough," thoroughly deserve to be branded as traitors to the working class. What, after all, do these "Socialists" say? They say: "We must not let the millionaires be inconvenienced, rather let millions of workers starve."

The capitalist world is decaying and the stench of its corpse contaminates all those who voluntarily or involuntarily serve its inhuman interests, its already impotent striving to transmute the flesh of the workers and peasants into gold. The "lip-service Socialists" whom the working class, until recently, regarded as its friends and leaders, are also rapidly decaying.

Now the workers of the world understand more and more clearly that they have only one friend, one teacher and leader who will not betray them, will not sell them, and that this leader lives and works in the Union of Soviet Socialist Republics; that he is not an individual, but a vast body of millions firmly welded by the consciousness of their historical class tasks.

There are people in the Soviet Union who declare, "Our country is living in an epoch of unprecedented growth of creative energy," but immediately afterwards they begin to plead for the slackening of this energy. They do this for different reasons, but on the whole their motif is distrust of the power of the working class. Evidently, the reflection of this doubt and distrust penetrates among the workers, for I some-times receive, together with the collective letters from heroes of socialist competition, letters from individuals which plainly ring with the distrust of people in their own strength, with scepticism as to the possibility of finishing the great work begun, *i.e.*, doubt of the inevitability of victory. I would re-mind these people of what Comrade Stalin said in one of his speeches, which he always builds upon verified facts, on the facts of the creativeness of many millions of rank and file, "common" labourers, the builders of socialism. He said: "We have all the objective conditions necessary for victory. The rest depends on our will, on our intelligence." What do his words mean?

They mean that you, comrades, have taken power in the richest country in the world, a country whose known natural wealth is immense—and yet we do not know the real measure of it, and have only begun to use an insignificant part of it. Our scientists, exploring the depths of the earth, almost every day discover new deposits of coal and ores, and fertiliser which we need to increase the fertility of our fields. It is as if the earth feels that a legitimate, real, and wise master has arisen and, opening her secret chests, displays her treasures before him.

From the simplest button and match to the combine and the aeroplane, everything is created by man. Human labour energy solves all the secrets of life, all its riddles. This means all we have to do is develop and increase this energy, and that is up to you!

The capitalist world, the world of piratical individualists, did not have to concern itself very much about exploring and discovering the treasures of the earth—the robbers preferred to grow rich by sapping the vital, cheap power of the workers. You are building a state in which violence, the senseless waste of human energy on insane luxury, the maintenance of huge armies, the waste of valuable metals in manufacturing weapons for mass murder, for war, will be impossible. You are building up a state in which all will have an equal right to develop their talents and abilities, in which the path to science and art is open wide for every one; a state in which there is no master class, but in which every one is master on a par with every one else.

This is a great, a difficult task, and of course I know that you are having a hard time. But you are free to make your life easier, and only you yourselves can do this. There is still much that you lack, but only you yourselves can produce that which you lack. Within your midst, enemies, people of the old world, are still whining and groaning, whispering to you despicable, philistine ideas, trying to make you distrustful of the greatness of your work, to raise doubts in your minds as to the inevitability of your victory. Only you can, and must, destroy this abomination, these wretched remnants of the old world.

Your power is indestructible, comrades. You have proved this in the Civil War, in class battles, and you are daily proving this by your heroic work. Your power is indestructible and assures you victory over all obstacles. You must overcome them all, and you are overcoming them. I warmly press your powerful hands.

1931

ON ANECDOTES

WE know that by its prolonged and continuous pressure upon the individual in all spheres, the bourgeois state creates a type of man whose profession it is to reconcile social contradictions.

This type is produced by the natural need of the philistine for some defence against the internal poisons which his unhealthy organism distils. He is "well-read," and is able more or less skilfully to compose ideas—and to decompose them when they contradict the philosophical precepts of the philistine outlook. We know that the philistine has a dual character, and cannot help having a dual character: in practical life he is a coarse and cynical materialist; in theory he is an idealist.

And it is to conceal this small but quite obvious contradiction that the reconciler of all sorts of contradictions is produced. It is his function to divert the attention of all people in general from reality, and especially of those who would honestly like to analyse the intricate complexity of ideas which try not only to justify but to lend permanent legitimacy to the philistine in general, and in particular to the "freethinking" philistine, who claims to be "spiritually" independent of the influence of reality. The chief method of diverting attention is to plunge the mind into the realm of "eternal mysteries." Although these mysteries are admitted to be incomprehensible, assiduous efforts are made to explain them with the help of "speculative thought"; and sometimes the reconciler will endeavour to explain them not because it is his function to do so, and not from mental curiosity, but from force of professional habit, and frequently because he has "nothing better to do."

The freethinking reconciler of social contradictions plunges into the realm of "eternal mysteries" from the viewpoint of the following: "We have learnt to know something, but we do not know how far what we know is authentic; we do not know what is concealed behind what we know, yet that which is concealed is the chief thing we ought to know. Who or what originated everything that exists, and how? And why was it originated? Everything—including thought—proceeds from the unknown. But does the unknown know doubt in the meaning of its existence? Do the Platonic ideas include the ideas: gramophone, trousers, machine gun, skis, turret lathe, tobacco pipe, sewing machine, tubercular bacillus, soap, flat-iron? Did my ego exist before my birth, and what will it experience after my death? Does a man sit on a stone, a chair, or on his buttocks; and what *rôle* does the terrestrial globe play in the act?"

The number of questions of this kind is endless; and many people of the type mentioned believe that by finding answers to such questions they are "adding depth to our knowledge of the meaning of being" and are also exposing errors of thought.*

These questions occupy the attention of the bigger birds—the crows, so to speak, not the rooks, magpies, and ravens.

---

* Those who think that I scoff at philosophy are mistaken. No, I am for philosophy; but for a philosophy that proceeds from below, from the earth, from the processes of work, which, by studying the phenomena of nature, places its forces at the service of mankind. I am convinced that thought is inseparably bound up with work, and I am no believer in thought done in a motionless state—sitting or lying down.

Culture and the People

The smaller "unfeathered bipeds" keep closer to philistine reality, and obscure its despicable meaning to the best of their ability.

The majority of them are scoundrels by nature, but humanists by conviction. They may be active members of the Society for the Prevention of Cruelty to Animals, but they look on indifferently while the police beat up workers in the streets of civilised European cities. They may protest against vivisection, defending the lives of rabbits, dogs, and guinea-pigs, yet they can argue the inevitability of imperialist wars, which exterminate tens of millions of people, and justify the barbarous colonial policy of the capitalist states; and they can, at the behest of their masters, incite the petty bourgeoisie of Europe to interfere in the Soviet Union and to commit terrorist acts against the Bolsheviks. In general they are "shamefully indifferent to good and evil," but in their work on the banker-owned newspapers they will preach some kind of "good," such as fascism, and "expose evil," that is, Communism.

The bosses feed them fairly well, and command: "Manufacture public opinion!" And they obediently set to work fabricating stories that in the Soviet Union the working people are yearning to have a tsar on their backs again, or a nice little parliament with bankers and manufacturers. These philistines try to prove that there is a breed of people who find life dull when they are not being beaten; that these people love suffering, as was shown by Dostoyevsky; that the more they are inflicted with boils the better they like it; that their patience is simply amazing. It is true that for four years, almost with naked hands, they patiently and perseveringly hammered at the armies of skilled generals and military ex-

140

perts and at the troops of the European bourgeoisie. But this fact is not mentioned.

These scribblers are very fond of recounting petty, vulgar, stupid, and preposterous anecdotes, which may be picked up and which are bound to be produced in a country where one hundred and sixty million people, the majority of them not very literate, have been set in motion.

These people have audaciously decided to create a new, socialist society. This work has never been undertaken before; they have nobody to learn from, they are suffering from a shortage of labour power; and, generally, the situation is such as to offer plenty of scope for the invention of all sorts of stupid anecdotes.

However, anecdotes, even by the hundred and thousand, have never noticeably retarded the development of a historical process. But the pirates of the pen and scoundrels of the bourgeois press are compelled by their bosses to make an effort to prove that anecdotes can retard and even completely halt the march of history. My own opinion on this subject is as follows: if an anecdote is witty it adorns history, as a well-executed miniature adorns the pages of a chronicle; but if the anecdote is ugly, vulgar, and stupid, its author very likely is also ugly.

An article appeared in *Pravda* (No. 254), entitled, "Without Revolutionary Theory There Can Be No Revolutionary Practice." That is true, and it should be repeated in various forms as often as possible. The article would have been even more instructive, impressive, and convincing if it had mentioned that revolutionary theory does not come "from the mind," or from "boredom with life," as is believed by certain naïve people, or people who pretend to be naïve but who are in reality rogues. Naïve people should be reminded that the theory of Leninism is founded on the facts of everyday, historical, labour practice, that it is deeply rooted in the soil and in the history of the long struggle of the working people to escape from the iron net of capitalism. People who have derived this simple truth from books, think that it is easy to grasp. But simple ideas are the wisest ideas, and are therefore the most difficult. Man's mind has been contaminated with numerous ideas which are fantastic and false but which are attractively dressed in fine words and therefore appeal to the mind. There is a proverb to the effect that, "Dirty linen clings to the skin."

The idea of a social revolution is a very simple one, and its truth is quite obvious. But this idea must penetrate the minds of the working people, who have been trained for centuries in the superstitions of a bestial, philistine individualism, skilfully wrapped up in grandiloquent phraseology. Moreover, one may not believe in God, yet—by the force of the traditions of our grandfathers and grandmothers, fathers and mothers— think about life ecclesiastically, that is, falsely.

The people who live by arduous physical toil have been trained for thousands of years to believe in a "destiny" that rules omnipotently over us, in a kingdom in heaven and in the unrestricted power of the kings on earth; they have been trained to be passive and submissive, although it is they and their labour that constitute the force which has constantly altered the forms of social life of their masters, and which has created culture. Some of the more active individuals, having managed to escape from the clutches of brutalising toil and poverty, joined the ranks of the plunderers of the masses. They had very weighty grounds for believing that life is determined by those who are cunning and shameless and therefore rich. They fostered in the masses the belief in a god who confers divinity and riches. There never has been a dictator who did not rely upon the church, nor a religion which did not serve the dictatorship of the rich over the working people.

All this is already known to millions of workers, but not to all. There are tens of thousands of young peasants active in our Soviet life who have not a very clear idea of the growth of revolutionary theory, or of the facts from which it has sprung. These young people should be made acquainted with the development of agriculture from primitive times to our day, with the development of science, technology, and industry, and with the history of the filthy and bloody practices of the philistines. Our young people should be acquainted with the "History of Mills and Factories," the "History of the Civil War," and of the first great victory of revolutionary theory over the filthy and bloody practices of the philistines. Our young people should also be acquainted with the affairs of current life, that is, with the history of their heroic labour. There may be youngsters among them to whom the stormy current of life is so incomprehensible as to cause them to ask: "What is the good of it?"

This question—"What is the good of it?"—has been put to me twice in its literal form and dozens of times in less definite forms. It is asked by young people who may be divided into two groups: those who are tired of "ideology" and would like, as one of them writes, to see "grass growing in the fields instead of nails, and the peasant embracing the peasant woman instead of a tractor." The second group consists of young people who are convinced of their own genius and are certain that they are "capable of solving all the problems of modern life, without referring to the past, which you recommend us to study because you are an old man and the past is precious to you, but which we do not feel and do not accept." Among this group there is a young blade who prefers ungrammatical language to the Russian language, and who argues as follows: "I have still to be convinced that study is always useful, and that it is not a habit of accumulating knowledge of unnecessary facts of life." And one man, scarcely a youngster, very irate, and anonymous, writes: "You are no longer an artist but a didactic old man; and old men are ambitious and love to teach, even though there is nobody to listen to them any longer in a country where life is governed by illiterate house porters and cooks...."

I shall supplement this description of the sentiments of my correspondents by the following. Some time ago I read a small book which cost ten kopeks and which contained a discussion between a professor and a student. The professor argued that only when we have mastered man's scientific experience and the history of his intellectual growth can we rapidly and successfully further scientific knowledge. The student objected that the stormy current of life and the work of construction required only an ability to apply ready-made formulas, and that all that was needed was a technical handbook; and "as to a knowledge of the profundities of scientific thought, that can be postponed to the future when more free time will be available for study." Unfortunately, the professor agreed with the student, and even passed him in the examination, thus allowing a half-educated man to occupy responsible posts and no doubt to commit blunder after blunder and to cause damage to the state.

The title "ambitious old man" is not new to me; it was conferred upon me long ago by the émigré press. And as to being called didactic, that rank was conferred upon me some thirty years ago. I do not hold myself to blame for being old; in my opinion, old age is not a crime, but something inevitable and very unpleasant. I should mention that I have no particular sympathy for the old-man tribe: I learnt in my youth that when they grow old many people acquire a thick coat of the wool, and even the bristle, of human "wisdom," that they become intolerant, importunate, and authoritative, and insist on their statements being accepted as axioms that require no proof and are above all criticism.

The young blades and geniuses may think that I say this with the object of pandering to their mood of excessive and illiterate criticism. But no. I do so for greater convenience in the fight, in order to give them a thorough trouncing to the best of my senile ability. I know that farmyard cocks who imagine they are eagles will never fly higher than the fence—but why, by one's silence, encourage the sterile attempts of certain young men to lift themselves by their own bootstraps?

To think that "the past is precious" to me is sheer ignorance. If it were, my guiding principle would be: "After me, the deluge"—and I would be in another camp, not in a camp where, apart from my direct duties as a writer, I have to act as a sanitary man and attempt to sweep life clean of all sorts of contaminating filth and rubbish.

It is this sanitary work that explains my tendency to be didactic referred to by my anonymous correspondent—that tendency to teach which is supposed to be inappropriate and even harmful in a writer of stories and novels. I know of no art which is not didactic, and I do not think that didacticism

145

is capable of diminishing the influence of art upon the imagination, mind, and will of the reader.

I personally have been learning all my life and continue to learn. I have learnt from Shakespeare and Cervantes, from August Bebel and Bismarck, from Leo Tolstoy and Vladimir Lenin, from Schopenhauer and Mechnikov, from Flaubert and Darwin, from Stendhal and Haeckel; I have learnt from Marx and also from the Bible; I have learnt from the anarchists Kropotkin and Stirner and from the "Church Fathers"; I have learnt from folklore and from carpenters, shepherds, factory workers, and from the thousands of other people among whom I have passed the half century of my conscious life. I do not find that anything superfluous was taught me in the school I am now finishing. While continuing to learn from Lenin and his disciples, I feel that I am at the same time learning from our not very highly educated shock workers and from the very highly educated Spengler. I am also learning something from my correspondents. This highly variegated course in knowledge I would call learning from realities, and I want to say that I consider my right to teach sufficiently well founded.

Several of my correspondents advise me: "Take a staff and a wallet; set out on foot and see for yourself. . . ." That I will not do; I have no time for such wanderings. I have wandered enough in my time, and I know very well under what intolerable conditions, in what poverty the peasants live. I know that fifty years ago there were many masters to batten on the peasant, but nobody to teach him. And in all the thousands of years he himself had learnt nothing.

Now he has a splendid teacher—the Communist worker—who has replaced the wooden plough by the tractor, the scythe and sickle by the harvester combine. He is relieving the peasant from inhuman toil and poverty and from the ancient "power of the soil" which held the mind of the peasant in superstitious darkness and in ignorance so profound as to deform his soul. I know how rapidly literacy is spreading among the peasantry, and with it a sense of human dignity and of the truth of collectivism.

Of course, there is a black sheep in every family; and as we have a family of one hundred and sixty million, it is only natural that there should be many black sheep in it. The black sheep is conceited and easily offended. He thinks himself unique, and he has reason to think so, of course, seeing that he is a black sheep.

The chief feature of the black-sheep mentality is a laziness of mind, an unwillingness to learn and know, a smug satisfaction or contentment with paucity of knowledge. It is usually called by one word: stupidity.

For example, one of these smug people writes:

If reality runs counter to my art, I have the right to reject it. It was Dostoyevsky, I think, who said that man is a creature of fantasy, and he was right. I value my fantasy higher than all your achievements, your Dnieper power stations, Magnitogorsk steel works, and Nizhni-Novogorod automobile works.

It is useless to argue with such a genius of a black sheep, because evidently he is constitutionally incapable of realising that all imagination is founded upon reality, and that a man can invent nothing unless he bases himself on something that was done before him, either in his interests or against his interests. One need not deny that "man is a creature of fantasy"; but if so he must be looked at from afar, from the "depths

147

of the cosmos," even as a creature who arose and grew up on one insignificant point of the universe, and who on this point, in the course of tens of thousands of years, by incredible effort, by arduous physical toil and intense creative effort, has achieved incredible successes. The most astonishing thing he has achieved is his science, whose audacious action knows no limits. Then there is his technology, which arose from science and which is overcoming the inertness of matter with greater and greater ease. Then there is his art, which enables him to turn words, sounds, colours, stone, and metal into images, compositions, and forms of ideal beauty and potency.

Regarded in this way man really is a creature of fantasy, and the history of his work and of his creative cultural activity is the most fantastic thing that can generally be imagined. To appreciate this man in all his greatness one must remember that his name is mankind, and one must know the history of his struggle against nature and of the struggle of classes within mankind. But the "genius" of young people like the author quoted above is inevitably accompanied by a profound and murky ignorance.

The young man who is tired of ideology writes:

Perhaps I am lagging behind life, perhaps I have become divorced from realities, but I am very fond of Zhukovsky's translations, his tales and legends; I am very fond of the opera *Ruslan and Ludmilla* and of much else in which you will not find any ideology even under a magnifying glass.

He goes on to ask: "Would it not be a good thing to permit the publication of literature which has no trace of ideology?"

On Anecdotes

He likes the film *Fear*, which protects the foundations of the bourgeois family, he likes the "comedians Pat and Patachon; their idiotic antics always arouse laughter." He wants to see "grass growing in the fields instead of nails, and the peasant embracing the peasant woman instead of a a tractor."

The general purport of his missive can be reduced to two words: Enjoy yourselves!

I have not quoted this letter because I consider it sillier than the others of its type. No, there are some which are far sillier. The young man who is fatigued by ideology is not as naïve as he would like to make out, and he is not protesting against all ideology, but against one quite definite ideology. He himself is profoundly ideological, and his motto—Enjoy yourselves!—is the ancient motto of drones and parasites: let others work, we want to enjoy ourselves. As you see, he has a penchant for the Lake Poets as translated by Zhukovsky. Byron, who although a lord was a revolutionary, and who detested the triumphant philistinism of his times, wrote of the Lake Poets as follows:

> *I would not imitate the petty thought,*
> *Nor coin my self-love to so base a vice,*
> *For all the glory your conversion brought,*
> *Since gold alone should not have been its price.*

And again:

> *Your bays may hide the baldness of your brows—*
> *Perhaps some virtuous blushes; let them go—*
> *To you I envy neither fruit nor boughs—*
> *And for the fame you would engross below.*

Robert Southey, Wordsworth, Coleridge, and the other poets

of the Lake School were admirers of Lord Castlereagh; but this is what Byron wrote of Castlereagh:

> *Cold-blooded, smooth-faced, placid miscreant!*
> *Dabbling its sleek young hands in Erin's gore,*
> *And thus for wider carnage taught to pant,*
> *Transferr'd to gorge upon a sister shore,*
> *The vulgarest tool that Tyranny could want,*
> *With just enough of talent, and no more,*
> *To lengthen fetters by another fix'd,*
> *And offer poison long already mix'd.*

There is one, but not unimportant, thing that can be said in favour of the Lake Poets. They knew how to make excellent use of the material of oral folklore. They thus considerably enriched the English language, as the historians of literature tell us, not forgetting to add, however, that Southey, Wordsworth, and Coleridge were mediocre poets. It is possible that in making use of the material of folklore, the greatest of our poets, Pushkin, followed their example. But a very essential difference in "taste" and attitude towards the material should be noted.

The Lake Poets avoided such themes as "The Priest and his Man, Balda." Pushkin never distorted the meaning of folk tales, whereas Wordsworth and his group borrowed from folklore its "supernatural" and "miraculous" themes, ideas, and superstitions, which had been introduced into healthy and pagan art by church hypocrisy. By giving their own interpretations to this ecclesiastical material, they acted as reconcilers of social contradictions. Wordsworth was "hostile to and even contemptuous of reason." Coleridge in his youth was a liberal, and later a disciple of the German mystic, Jakob Boehm, and a reactionary. Southey also began as a radical, but later became notorious for his savage hatred of Byron and Shelley, and finally sank to such depths of reactionary superstition that even Macaulay the historian, a conservative, sharply criticised his *Conversations.*

All these people are infected by the Lutheran precept that reason is the "whore of the devil," the precept of the Saxon peasant whose forefathers had lived for centuries under the incredibly bloodthirsty yoke of small princes, the church, the barons, and the landed gentry.

It was this yoke that inspired Luther's fanatical doctrine, the essence of which is: "The Christian must be absolutely passive, he must suffer in patience and shun the benefits of this life and think only of laying up treasures in heaven. The Christian must suffer and not show the least resistance, even if he is being skinned alive. He is indifferent to everything mundane. He will permit himself to be robbed, hacked, and tortured, for he is a martyr on earth." And when the peasantry, led by Thomas Münzer, Bender Heiler, and other of their own leaders, rose against the oppressors, Luther cried to the barons and the churchmen: "Save yourselves! Flog, thrash, and strangle the peasants for all you are worth! Destroy them like mad dogs."

That is the source from which the poets, so beloved of the young man who is fatigued by the ideology of the working class, drew their ideology. It remains for me to say a few words about Zhukovsky. Like Wordsworth and Robert Southey, he was a "court" poet, a poet laureate. He was the tutor of Alexander II, son of Nicholas I, and the author of an article in which he advocated and justified capital punishment. A sentimental reactionary, he possessed the talent of relating strange things in verse, but he was not a very great poet.

And so we see that it is not every ideology that fatigues the young man, but only one definite ideology, with which apparently he is poorly acquainted. It is quite possible that his penchant for the ballads of the Lake Poets and for legends and fables is due not to class taste, but to ignorance. He evidently does not know that the lovely words of ballads, fables, and legends also conceal a definite ideology, and sometimes a very putrid one, and that very likely cockroaches, rats, mosquitoes, and other parasites, too, possess the rudiments of a primitive "ideology"; for parasites are capable of certain ideas, founded on experience, *e.g.*, that land is firmer than water, that iron is inedible, and that the blood of man is nourishing. Most likely only idiots and cretins are unable to think ideologically, but it is not of them we are speaking.

It need hardly be said that I am not against people enjoying themselves. But under the conditions of our life enjoyment needs certain limitations: "An hour for amusement, all else for work."

It seems to me that if some are to amuse themselves with the charms of the verbal creations of reactionaries, class enemies of the working people, while others are to be constantly and indefatigably engaged in shock work devoted to the development of a new, socialist culture that will emancipate humanity, the result of such a contradiction will be that the former will be absolutely superfluous in our workers' world.

Furthermore, it is my belief that this world is interesting enough and rich enough in "amusements." For example, Gandhi and MacDonald are comedians just as amusing as Pat and Patachon, and the misdeeds of the villains of real life far surpass those of the villains in the movies. I repeat that, in general, reality has always served as the basis of inventions and fantasies; and that it is of greater interest and practical value not to study it from cinema films but from the acts of such gentlemen as Churchill, Chamberlain, Baldwin, and similar "heroes of our times." It is of greater value and interest because the aforesaid gentlemen, in view of their obvious inclination for political hooliganism, might raise a few bumps on the head of the young man who is tired of ideology. These gentlemen will not hesitate to do so if the young man keeps gazing at the crows, an occupation, I hope, which is not congenial to more than a few of the citizens of the Soviet Union. What these few citizens think and write was thought of and written about far better and far more comprehensively at the beginning of the nineteenth century by people who at that time were also "tired" of the revolutionary ideology of the materialists of the "age of enlightenment"; and what the "tired ones" wrote of then was a fanatical, ecclesiastical, counter-revolutionary ideology.

As to the nails which are supposed to be growing in our fields, I can say nothing about them: I have never seen any such nails or any such fields. The writer of the letter was no doubt joking. But as regards the peasant, I can say with absolute certainty that even in our day, but still more somewhat later—when, having ceased to feel himself a peasant, he will regard himself as a socialist and the master of his country— he will most certainly embrace the peasant woman; and she will embrace him too. That is their mutual, biological and, as we know, most pleasant duty.

Even monks, the ideologists of asceticism, could testify on the basis of their personal experience that even asceticism is

no hindrance to the performance of this duty. Even homo-
sexualists, who retreat from this duty, explain this retreat ideologically, or by their attraction for the aestheticism of Hellen-
ism, or else by the simple fact that in bourgeois society it is
cheaper to keep a man than a woman. So there is "ideology"
everywhere, young man. It has never prevented people from
performing their "duty," and ever since ancient times has encouraged the performance in verse and prose, colour and
dance. Philistine reality tells us that in bourgeois society this
duty is increasingly assuming the form and character of a disgusting perversion and the degradation of the human being—
woman. While "protecting family life" in the cinema, in actual
life the philistine is more and more compelling women to re-
sort in self-defence to the revolver and carbonic acid, as is
related daily and in sadistic detail in the bourgeois press by the
reporters—the people we spoke about at the beginning of this
article.

These people cannot claim our sympathy, of course, but they
are very useful, because they are naturalists. Their original
ancestor was Ham, the smart lad who uncovered the nakedness
of his drunken father. They are also engaged in uncovering
the disgusting nakedness of their father—their class—by filling
the columns of bourgeois newspapers with circumstantial descriptions of the disintegrating family in petty bourgeois society, and with reports of murders, suicides, and various forms
of robbery, forgery, and swindling. It is their profession to
rake up the blood, filth, and garbage of petty-bourgeois life;
they are highly absorbed by this profession, and they present
us with a broad and very vivid picture of the rottenness and
decay of European bourgeois culture. They too are rotten—
but they are useful rotters, for their "naturalism" throws a fairly

154

strong light on realities. The testimony of these people must be studied attentively, but they should not be imitated, for they are soulless individuals who regard the drama of their petty-bourgeois mode of life as material which can be bought and sold to ensure the "naturalist" a certain amount of grub.

Our Soviet life still contains survivals of the old order, but they are rapidly disappearing. We have our own peculiar "naturalists," and they too write. I hesitate to call them descendants of Ham, for it sometimes seems to me that they stress the filth and vileness of life from hygienic motives, from a desire to give the final blow to the dying order and to eject it from our life altogether. But, as I say, they overlook the political side.

They are keen observers and apparently faithful reporters. For example, in the book of one competent writer I find the following statement: "Recently, a man with a beard was given a job on a provincial political educational department owing to a misunderstanding; he was formerly a graveyard watchman."

Very funny, isn't it? And it is possibly true. We are experiencing a shortage of forces everywhere, and a graveyard watchman might prove to be politically better educated than our author. But the foreign naturalists and the native ill-wishers of the workers' and peasants' government will most certainly draw a different conclusion from this anecdote, namely, that in the Soviet Union political education is in the hands of graveyard watchmen. In order to lend greater piquancy to the wretched anecdote, they may turn the watchman into a gravedigger. The philistines, our native ones and the old émigrés in Paris, Berlin, Prague, Sophia, and Belgrade, tickled by the Soviet writer, will exultantly ring each other up on the telephone, and shriek: "Have you read about the gravediggers? Ha, ha, that's a good one!"

I come across many such anecdotes in the books of our writers. But I will not quote them here, for I have no inclination to tickle the philistines with truths that may be pleasant to them and revive their despicable hopes.

A question that greatly interests me is: Whence this passion of our writers for the "truth" which is pleasant to the philistine? This "truth" is the product of his class creative activity. During a conversation with a certain author about his manuscript, which was almost entirely based on pessimistic anecdotes and on a hero who is tormented because he is unable to find a well-sounding name for himself, I asked him: "What interest is it to me, the reader, that some blockhead Semkov, instead of working and studying, keeps muttering: Semiokov, Sumrakov, Sumarokov?" The answer I got was: "I like people who live without action, within themselves, and who develop by their own forces, like you."

This is a very strange anecdote, because the gross and commonplace naturalism of the manuscript was in absolute contrast to the obvious romanticism of the morose and irate author. Verbally, he displayed this romanticism quite definitely, yet it seemed just grafted to his skin and did not proceed from within him. And, generally, it often seems to me that some of our young writers study not reality so much as Friedrich Schlegel, who one hundred and thirty-two years ago preached that "the human ego derives true satisfaction not from energetic activity, but from the divine art of passivity, from the absence of all activity, when it lives in 'self-enjoyment'; and the more it resembles a plant the better off it is. . . ."

This doctrine of purely passive romanticism cropped up

On Anecdotes

again and again, in the nineteenth and twentieth centuries, and often in curious forms, as in the case of Huysman's *Against the Grain* and of the over-praised Walt Whitman, and, finally, of the intolerably verbose Marcel Proust. It is very possible that the inclination for passive romanticism betrayed by a certain, scarcely considerable, number of our young writers is due to their emotional desire for active romanticism, revolutionary romanticism, the romanticism in which our life is so wonderfully rich, and which profoundly imbues the work of our young people, who are not creating a "legend," but are furthering the world cause of the emancipation of the working people. One may well grant, as we have already said, that young people note and heavily stress the anecdotal and ugly manifestations of the old order out of hatred for it, from sanitary motives, from a desire to destroy everything that prevents young people from acquiring a revolutionary, active romanticism. But this romanticism is achieved only by developing and deepening class consciousness, only by political self-education. Only under such conditions does the question—"What is the good of it all?" —fall away, and the young man acquire a clear idea of the high aim which the working class of the Union of Soviet Socialist Republics has set itself. That aim is the great and gleaming truth of which the working people of the whole world have dreamt from time immemorial, and which alone can emancipate them from a life of blood, filth, lies, and the stifling mesh of irreconcilable class antagonisms.

But the vile and despicable "truth" of the philistine has not yet perished; it still lives and exerts its influence on the minds of men who are tired of the revolutionary ideology of the working class. The descendants of Ham, the "naturalists," "penpirates," hirelings of the bankers, and generally, the petty peo-

157

ple who live by the principle, "After us, the deluge," make use of this truth in their vilification of the Soviet Union and socialism.

"Industrialisation," they say, "Five-Year Plan, Magnitostroy, Dnieprostroy, joining the river Moscow with the Volga—yet a graveyard watchman is imparting political education. And writer so-and-so, forgetting that his heroes are sailing down the Oka, describes a night on the Volga; and school teacher so-and-so has received no salary for three months. In the town of Okurovo the co-operative society funds have been embezzled by the manager. You are making blooming mills, tractors, and conveyors, yet pins, needles, and hairpins are sometimes nowhere to be found, you poor devils!" etc., etc.

And all this is true. But what would you have? There are plenty of truths like this still to be found between Vladivostok and Odessa, Erivan and Murmansk, Leningrad and Tashkent. These defects are not to be got rid of all at once. But, we are gradually getting rid of them; and when we do so, it is with a ruthless hand. Our enemies think they are putting our noses out of joint with these anecdotal truths. Let us leave them in the mists of self-deception, but let us see to it that the number of vulgar anecdotes is reduced. The philistine should not be fed even on the filth he likes. The number of anecdotes will rapidly diminish; all we have to do is grasp the truth that every one of us is answerable to the whole country and to every individual in it for everything we do. It is time we developed a sense of socialist responsibility and solidarity on a nation-wide scale. And together with this sense we should develop political tact, which will not permit us to invent anecdotes in life and literature, and will not permit us to console philistinism with proofs that it is still alive in our own breasts.

On Anecdotes

There is nothing worse than a man who is a socialist externally but not at heart. The future we are building to-day is stretching out to us its strong and generous hand. So much has already been done that it requires only a little more effort to make the great dictator of the Soviet Union—the working class —a power that will not be vanquished by any combination of the already tattered forces of its class enemies.

1931

THE OLD MAN AND THE NEW

THE nineteenth century received the high-sounding title, the "Age of Progress." The title was deserved. In that century, reason, scientifically investigating the phenomena of nature and subjugating its elemental forces to economic interests, reached unparalleled heights and created many "marvels of technique." In the study of organic life, reason discovered the invisible world of bacteria, a discovery which was not used to the fullest extent, owing to the shameful and cynical conservatism of social and class conditions. In the Russian translation of Wallace's book, *The Twentieth Century*, we find the following words: "In this century the eagle flight of thought majestically and proudly revealed its powers to man."

But side by side with scientific thought, another kind of thought was no less active. It created in the bourgeoisie the state of mind known as *weltschmertz*—the philosophy and poetry of pessimism. In 1812 Lord Byron published the first stanzas of *Childe Harold*, and soon after Giacomo Leopardi, Count Monaldo, philosopher and poet, began to preach that knowledge only betrayed the impotence of reason, that all was vanity, and that the only truths were suffering and death. The idea was not a new one; it had been beautifully formulated by Ecclesiastes, it had been preached by Buddha, and it had burdened the reason of Thomas More, Jean Jacques Rousseau, and many other great minds and talents. The revival of this idea by Byron and Leopardi can scarcely be attributed only to the

160

The Old Man and the New

despondency aroused in representatives of the feudal nobility by the victory of the bourgeoisie; but there is no doubt that, when the bourgeoisie fell heir to the land of the aristocrats, it also fell heir to some of its ideas—ideas have an obnoxious way of surviving the conditions which created them.

The tenacity of pessimism can well be explained by the fact that this philosophy is by its very nature profoundly conservative, and that, by affirming that life is meaningless, it fully satisfies not over-curious minds and consoles lovers of tranquillity. Its tenacity may also be attributed to the fact that the circle of consumers of ideas is very narrow, and not very rich in originality and boldness of thought.

In the nineteenth century the Germans were most assiduous in supplying Europe with pessimistic ideas. Not to mention the Buddhist philosophy of Schopenhauer and Hartmann, the anarchist Max Stirner, in his book, *The Ego and His Own*, is nothing but a profound pessimist. The same must be said of Friedrich Nietzsche, who expressed the bourgeois yearning for a "strong man"—a yearning which, retrogressing, sank from the glorified Friedrich the Great to Bismarck, to the half-insane Wilhelm II, in our day, to the obviously abnormal Hitler.

During the first twelve years it was Bonaparte, "the little corporal," who served the European bourgeoisie as a model of the "great man." The influence of his semi-fantastic biography on the thoughts and feelings of a number of generations of philistines has not yet been adequately investigated, although Bonaparte was the most convincing proof of the philistine's need to stake everything on a "hero," and of the inevitability of the hero's collapse.

As we know, the *rôle* of the "hero" as the creator of history was very eloquently, if rather hysterically, propounded by Carlyle. His conclusions were accepted; but this did not prevent the heroes diminishing to the dimensions of Clemenceau, Churchill, Woodrow Wilson, Chamberlain, and other "leaders of cultured humanity," as these people are called by their lackeys.

The attitude of the employers towards these heroes, who are their servants, is more restrained, for when the various groups of employers started the carnage of 1914-18, knowing that "war produces heroes," each expected to secure for itself an Alexander the Great, or a Tamerlane, or at least a Napoleon, but actually secured Joffres, Pershings, and Ludendorffs. To "return to our muttons," we should mention among the German pessimists Weininger, the author of a gloomy book called *Sex and Character*, and Spengler, the author of *The Decline of the West* and *Men and Technology*.

The "decline of the West," that is, its spiritual impoverishment, exhaustion of talents, paucity of organising ideas, are features that are peculiar not only to Europe, but to both the Americas and to the whole world. The bright stars in the bourgeois heaven have been extinguished!

The Forsytes in England, the Buddenbrooks in Germany, and the Babbitts in the United States are clearly incapable of producing "heroes," and are obliged to fashion them out of petty adventurers.

In the country where once the vague benignity of the optimist Dickens obscured the healthy criticism of Thackeray, the gloomy Thomas Hardy has recently passed away, and such malicious books, full of appalling despair, as Richard Aldington's *Death of a Hero* have now become possible. French literature in the twentieth century has not been capable even of such artistic generalisations as have been achieved by Galsworthy, Thomas Mann, and Sinclair Lewis. Romain Rolland, author of the magnificent epic, *Jean Christophe*, a man of honesty and courage, lives outside his country, from which he has been driven by the savage stupidity of the bourgeois. Thereby France is the loser, and the world of the working people the gainer.

Rentier France resembles a boa-constrictor, which, having swallowed too much food, is unable to digest it, and at the same time is afraid that all it has not managed to consume will be consumed by others of its kind. Of course, intellectual poverty does not prevent the customary and senseless striving of the profiteers to seize new stretches of fertile territory and to enslave people in the colonies. But the gold-fatty degeneration is weighing more and more heavily and disgustingly on the brain of the bourgeoisie. The spectacle presented by spiritually impoverished Europe is astonishing, although people are increasingly arising in it who are ashamed of living under the cynical conditions the profiteers have created, and who realise that the stake of the shopkeepers on a "hero," on individualism, has been lost.

The question—What did the social culture of Europe achieve in the nineteenth century?—can be answered only in one way, namely, that it grew so disgustingly rich, that it became obvious to all that its wealth was the cause of the unprecedented poverty of the working class. A gulf has been formed between the working class and the bourgeoisie so profound that the collapse of the bourgeoisie into this gulf has become absolutely inevitable.

And that is the right place for it, of course. Will "culture" suffer? Revolutions have never been pauses in the history of man's cultural development; revolution is a process that calls to life new creative forces.

The process of the cultural revolution is rapidly developing on the territory of the former Russia of the Romanov tsars and semi-literate merchants, who auctioned off the treasures of their country to the European capitalists and plundered the workers and peasants, who were under the sway of ignorant priests, extinguishers of reason.

I think that this is the place to refer to my own biography. It is one that entitles me to be considered an informed and truthful witness.

For nearly fifty years I have been observing the life of people of different classes. Not trusting too much my own impressions, I checked them by studying the history of my people and comparing it with the history of European peoples. I was sufficiently "objective" even when I felt that objectivism was retarding my grasp of the most simple "truths" of life and was distorting the straight-line development of my knowledge of the world.

It is not easy to understand that at the basis of objectivism lies a desire shared by the majority of people, if not to reconcile, at least to counter-balance facts that are intrinsically irreconcilable. This should be well understood by people of a country where the doctrine of compromise was invented, and where only a few intellectuals, experts in discussing the secrets of life, and only after the gruesome war of 1914-18, are beginning to understand that what is needed is not the reconciliation of contradictions, but the study of their causes.

I assert that the worker and peasant of tsarist Russia lived in an incomparably worse state than any of the labouring classes of Europe. Working people in Russia had fewer rights and were kept in a state of greater ignorance.

The pressure of the government and the church on man's will and reason was more severe, gross, and monstrous than in Europe. Nowhere did talented people perish in such numbers and so easily as on Russian soil. I am not one of the "blind patriots of the fatherland," and I am certain that I know the "soul of the people" well. It is a very "broad" and capacious soul, but it was saturated and poisoned by the dark and preposterous superstitions and the savage prejudices of primitive conditions of life. Incidentally, it should be studied not from Turgenev, Tolstoy, or Dostoyevsky, but from its folklore, its songs, fables, proverbs, and legends, from its domestic and religious rites, its sects and handicrafts, and its work in the realm of art industry. This alone will give a full and weighty picture of the appalling darkness of the people, and at the same time of their astonishing, variegated, and profound talents.

In the first half of the nineteenth century the writers coming from the nobility depicted the peasantry—the "god-fearing" people—with compassion as soft-hearted poets and dreamers who bore their fate submissively. The government had to be convinced that the peasant was a human being, that it was time to remove the yoke of slavery—serfdom—from his neck, and to give him the rudiments of an education. This propaganda of primitive humanitarianism was continued by the bourgeois intellectuals in the second half of the century, and they painted the muzhik in the same bright and tender hues in which he was depicted by Turgenev, Tolstoy, and others. It may be said that the nobles wanted to have a literate muzhik only so as to have a somewhat more productive form of labour power, and

165

the bourgeoisie in order to use this power in its struggle against the autocracy.

With the development of industry at the end of the century, the Russian bourgeoisie began to produce "legal Marxists"—a sort of domestic fowl of philistinism, like the geese that are said to have saved Rome. They talked of getting the poetical muzhik "stewed" in the "kettle of the factory." It was at this same time that the autocratic government, "in compliance with the demand of the times," introduced, in opposition to the *zemstvo* schools, which were secular, parochial schools in which the village priests taught. With all this, the attitude of literature towards the muzhik underwent a sharp change: the mild dreamer and poet disappeared, and his place was taken by the savage, tipsy, and bizarre "muzhiks" of Chekhov, Bunin, and other writers.

I am not inclined to think that such a change of type took place in reality, but it is certainly to be found in the literature of the early part of the twentieth century. This literary transformation does not speak very convincingly in favour of the social independence of art; but it does very positively indicate a harmonious combination of the voice of the "free thinking individuality" and the voice of his class, and the replacement of the idea of persuading by the idea of gratifying.

And so, it was not a very appealing literary portrait of the muzhik that the bourgeoisie had before it in the twentieth century. In 1905, 1906, and 1907, the original of this portrait, having decided to free the land for himself, began to burn down the mansions of the gentry; but his attitude towards the workers, the "strikers," was a grumpy and not very trustful one. However, in 1917 he came to understand the truth about the working class and, as we know, plunging his bayonet into the ground he refused to go on destroying German workers and peasants.

We also know that the German army, on the plea of the "right of conquest," despoiled the Russian muzhik rather thoroughly, and that the European capitalists, outraged at his unusual action, unanimously sent their own muzhiks and workers to subdue and exterminate the refractory Russians. This despicable business was supported by the majority of the Russian liberal and radical intellectuals; they came to the defence of capitalism, sabotaged the Soviet government, plotted against it, and resorted to acts of terrorism against the leaders of the workers and peasants. The shot fired at Lenin brought home to the masses of workers and peasants who their true friend and leader was, and how vile their enemies were, and aroused an attitude of hostility towards this section of the intelligentsia— an attitude justified by their treachery. The European intellectuals might well draw a lesson from this.

Since then fifteen years have elapsed.

What has been accomplished in the Soviet Union during this interval? I shall not speak of the tremendous work done in the industrial equipment of a country that was technically backward, a country whose primitive industry was completely shattered by the general European capitalist war and then by the war of the working class against the native savages and European savages, a war in which the workers fought for the right to culture—and the intellectuals for the right of the bourgeoisie to rob.

I shall point to the broad development—during these fifteen years—of universities and scientific research institutes, to the big discoveries of mineral wealth, enough to ensure the economic and cultural progress of the country for many centuries to come. All this is well known. These achievements of reason and will power are not seen only by those who have been blinded by the bestial interests and inhuman prejudices of their class. They are not seen by those who will not see them, and by journalists whom their bosses have forbidden to see the truth.

In the Soviet Union there is only one master—that is the basis of its achievements, and it is that which distinguishes it from bourgeois states. The master is the workers' and peasants' state, guided by the organisation of Lenin's disciples. The aim they have set themselves is a perfectly clear one, namely, to create for each of the units in the multi-national population of one hundred sixty million people, conditions that will favour the growth of its talents and faculties. In other words, to set this vast quantity of potential and passive neuro-cerebral energy into active motion, to awaken its creative faculties. Is this possible?

It is being done. The masses, to whom all the doors of culture have been opened, are producing from their midst tens of thousands of talented young people in all fields—science, technology, art, and administration.

Our life and work are, of course, not free from mistakes; but the property instinct, the stupidity, laziness, and other vices inherited from past centuries cannot be eliminated in fifteen years. Yet one must be crazy, or crazed by resentment, to deny the incontestable fact that the distance which separates the younger generation of European workers from the unquestionable achievements of human culture is speedily diminishing in the Soviet Union.

Taking as a basis everything that is of lasting value in the old culture, the peoples of the Soviet Union are boldly developing their own, yet generally human, values. And anybody can convince himself of this who will examine the young literature and music of the national minorities of the Soviet Union.

Mention should be made of the emancipation of the women of the Tyurkic and Tyurko-Finnish tribes, their striving towards new social forms and activity.

Legislation in the Soviet Union originates and springs from the masses of working people; it is based upon their labour experience and the various changes in labour; the Council of People's Commissars only lends form to this experience and these laws, and can do so only in the interests of the working people—for there is no other master in the country.

In all other parts of the world laws fall like a hail of stones from above, and they all have two purposes: to exploit the labour energy of the working people, and to prevent the transformation of physical energy into intellectual energy. If the resources the bourgeoisie spends on armaments for the purposes of mutual robbery were devoted to public education, the frightful countenance of the bourgeois world would perhaps not be so abhorrent. The hatred of the bourgeoisie for the Soviet Union compels the latter, too, to devote time and metal to armaments—this must be regarded as another crime of the European bourgeoisie against its workers and peasants.

Nobody can point to a single decree of the Council of People's Commissars which was not designed to meet the cultural demands and needs of the working people. Leningrad is being reconstructed. The conferences on the subject are attended by doctors, artists, sanitary authorities, architects, writers and, of course, workers—representatives from the factories. As far as I am aware this practice does not exist anywhere in Europe.

With a captiousness which in my opinion is excessive and

169

even prejudicial, for it arouses impracticable hopes in the mind of the philistine, the Soviet press exposes mistakes in work and the vices and follies of the old order. This is something the bourgeois press dare not do; instead it corrupts the minds of its uncultured readers with circumstantial and sadistic descriptions of murders, or with enticing stories of adroit swindlers.

During the past fifteen years the ranks of the workers and peasants have produced thousands of inventors, and are continuing to produce them. They are saving many millions of rubles annually for the Soviet Union and are gradually relieving the population of the necessity of imports.

The worker who feels that he is the master of industry naturally develops a sense of his responsibility to the country, and this induces him to strive to improve the quality of the articles he produces and to reduce their cost.

Before the Revolution the peasant worked under conditions that were reminiscent of the seventeenth century; he was completely dependent on the caprices of nature, on his impoverished land, which was broken up into separate tiny strips. Now he is rapidly resorting to the use of tractors, seed-drills, and harvester combines; he makes extensive use of fertilisers, and he has the services of twenty-six scientific research institutes at his disposal. A man who had never had the least idea of science, he is now obtaining a demonstration of its cogency and of the power of human thought.

The village youth who comes to work in a factory built in accordance with the latest and most perfected achievements of technology, finds himself in a world of phenomena that astounds his imagination, awakens his mind, and rids it of ancient and savage superstitions and prejudices. He sees the working of reason embodied in complex machinery and lathes. From inexperience he may, of course, damage one thing or another, but the loss he causes is compensated by the growth of his mind. He sees that the masters of the factory are workers like himself, that the young engineer is a son of a worker or a peasant. He very soon arrives at the conclusion that the factory is a school that affords him the opportunity of freely developing his abilities. His neuro-cerebral energy, on which our faculty of investigating and knowing the phenomena of the world depends, is powerfully stimulated by a complex of conditions which were utterly unknown to his father.

He visits theatres that are acknowledged to be the best in Europe; he reads the classical literature of Europe and old Russia; he attends concerts, frequents museums, and studies his country as it has never been studied before.

Comrade Kuibyshev recently invited the members of the Young Communist League to take part in the search for deposits of metals and non-metallic minerals all over the country. That means that tens of thousands of young people will be working under the guidance of the finest geologists in the Soviet Union to enrich the industry of their country with discoveries of new deposits of raw material and to enrich themselves with new experience. The organisation of an army for such purposes in capitalist countries is unthinkable and, what is more, there is nothing to search for in these countries, which have been pillaged by the irresponsible administration of the capitalists. Should the European pirates attempt a marauding raid on the Soviet Union, their armies will encounter fighters each of whom knows very well what he has to defend.

In their cynical game the capitalists rely on the stupidity of the masses; but in the Soviet Union the working masses are being trained in the knowledge of their right to rule. A new type of man is springing up in the Soviet Union, and his characteristics may already be defined without fear of error.

He possesses a faith in the organising power of reason, a faith that has been lost by the European intellectuals, who have been exhausted by the sterile labour of reconciling class contradictions. He is conscious of being the builder of a new world, and although his conditions of life are still arduous, he knows that it is his aim and the purposes of his rational will to create different conditions—and he has no grounds for pessimism. He is young historically as well as biologically.

He is a force that has only just become aware of its path and purpose in history, and he is performing his task of cultural development with all the courage inherent in a force which has just begun to function and which is guided by a simple and clear precept. He is amused to hear the cries and groans of the Spenglers, who are terrified at technology, for he knows very well that technology has never yet worked in the interests of the cultural development of hundreds of millions of people enslaved by physical toil. He perceives that the bourgeoisie has shamefully miscalculated in basing itself on individualism, that generally it has not furthered the development of the individuality, but has selfishly restricted its development by ideas that overtly or covertly claimed, as an "eternal truth," that its power did not extend to the majority of people.

While rejecting the bestial individualism of the bourgeoisie, the new man perfectly understands the profound integrality of the individuality which is closely bound up with the collective body; he himself is such an individuality that freely draws its energy and inspiration from the masses, in the process of the labour of the masses. Capitalism has led mankind into anarchy, and is threatening to plunge humanity into a frightful catastrophe.—That is clear to every honest man.

The aim of the old world is, by physical and moral violence to restore the old, rotten, inhuman "order," without which capitalism cannot exist.

The aim of the new world is to liberate the working people from the ancient superstitions and prejudices of race, nation, class, and religion, and to create a world-wide fraternal society, every member of which will work according to his ability and receive according to his needs.

1932

ABOUT "SOLDIERLY" IDEAS

RECENTLY, at a parade of the "Steel Helmets" (*Stahlhelm*) in Berlin, the president of the organisation, Seldte, a manufacturer of liqueurs, said:

> When the Stahlhelm marches, it means the regeneration of the German soldierly spirit. Soldierly ideas and soldierly affairs are again appreciated in Germany.

About thirty years ago somebody, I do not remember who, wrote a biography of the philosopher Fichte, in which he said:

> Germany is a country of philosophers; and while in France politics are made by lawyers, in Germany it is the philosophers who command the spirit of the nation.

But here we see that manufacturers of liqueurs have begun to make politics. Of course, this is not something new, and although it is a bad thing, it is quite natural in a state of capitalists. Still, a manufacturer of liqueurs is hardly a philosopher. A bourgeois philosopher, as we know, is a lover of wisdom, who reasons for the purpose of "explaining the world," or of explaining the technique of thinking in the world. This is his profession and, from the point of view of people engaged in the real work of changing the world, the bourgeois philosopher may be called—without any offence being intended—an "idler." The liqueur manufacturer is not a philosopher, but a man of affairs—of "soldierly" affairs.

174

About "Soldierly" Ideas

It is easy to picture to oneself what "soldierly" deeds mean; the bloody horrors of these "deeds" in 1914-18 have not quite been forgotten, as may be clearly seen from the mood of the broad masses, reflected in the recent anti-war congress in Amsterdam. Neither have the horrors of the foul European intervention in the Soviet Union been forgotten. Recently the destruction wrought by the Japanese in Chapei reminded us of "soldierly" deeds.

But what are "soldierly" ideas? As far as is known, the history of philosophy makes no mention of the existence of this variety, and there is every ground to assert that in general "soldierly" ideas are something impossible, because everywhere and always soldiers have been instructed "not to reason why," and whenever they did reason they were punished for it.

The training of soldiers in the tsarist army was copied entirely from Germany. The soldier had no right to answer the questions of his commander with a plain honest, "I don't know"; he was obliged to answer, "I cannot know." By these words the soldier was forced to renounce his ability and right to know anything that was in the least degree outside the range of the "Service Regulations," one of the most despicable documents created by bourgeois civilisation.

When a man was put in a soldier's uniform, it was impressed upon him not only that he was unworthy and had no business to know, but that by his very "nature" as a soldier he could not, was in fact unable to know anything outside the scope of rules of the service. The soldier of a bourgeois army is a man who is being deliberately stupefied by his class enemy, so as to ensure his—the worker's or peasant's—submissiveness to the rule of the bourgeoisie. The soldier of a European army is a man who lives in captivity, hypnotised by his enemies and doing their bidding for a paltry wage and a piece of rotten bread. At the same time soldiers are people; they have fathers and mothers, brothers and sisters who work and pay enormous taxes to clothe, arm, and feed their children and brothers during their service in the army. And when life becomes so hard for their fathers and brothers that they "revolt" against their ancient enemies, the soldiers are obliged to fire at the "insurgents." And they fire, too—so profound is the state of idiocy to which the capitalists have reduced them.

For more than half a year the clerks of the capitalists chattered in Geneva about disarmament. The soldiers of the European armies remained deaf and dumb as far as this chattering was concerned; yet they could have turned it into a serious business. They could have said something of very great moment apropos the ever increasing expenditures for armaments, of the senseless wastage of metal for cannon and tanks, of the new world carnage which the capitalists are preparing—and which will entail the transformation of millions of live and healthy people into corpses or invalids. But the soldier is made into a man who cannot know and who does not reason. The liqueur manufacturer lies: soldiers in the ranks have no "soldierly" ideas of any kind. But since there are quite a number of proletarians in the armies of the imperialists, the former are, of course, doing their proletarian, historically necessary work in the barracks; and the soldiers of the bourgeoisie are beginning to think.

There is but one army in the world whose members have the right and the duty to think, and this is our army, the Red Army. Any member of this army never says, "I cannot know"— he has the right and the duty to know everything. And he knows that which is essential: who, and where, his enemy is;

About "Soldierly" Ideas

that this enemy is the exploiter who wants to live off the labor of others, who wants to live for his own self alone, the rapacious life of a spider. A member of the Red Army is a citizen of his country, the owner and guard of his country and the builder of its future.

To the question—From which class are the members of the "Steel Helmets" chiefly recruited?—I received the following answer: "They are recruited mainly from among the children of those who were killed during the war of 1914-18, and they are the avengers of their fathers and of their outraged fatherland." There is certainly a great number of children of this type in France, and the governments of all the countries which participated in the World War are bringing up such "avengers." While inciting these "war-orphans" against other orphans, the lackeys of capital, the mercenary souls, the rogues of the press and the corsairs of the pen hide from the youth this clear and simple truth: that the hand which committed the murder is not as guilty as the odious head which instigated the murder. No one can deny this obvious fact, that the instigator is the capitalist, the worshipper of private property, a being deformed by insatiable cupidity, envy, and a senseless passion for accumulating money and objects; a being resembling a man, but losing more and more even the physical semblance of a normal human being.

The "war-orphans" and "avengers of their fathers" are like tin soldiers in the hands of a degenerate and vicious boy. Tired of his toys, he finds pleasure in tearing off the heads and legs of the tin soldiers. The difference between a tin soldier and an "avenger" is that, before the "avenger's" head is torn off, it is filled with poisonous rubbish. The "avenger" is made to believe that there is something called fatherland, and that he must

177

defend this fatherland which is entirely in the hands of irresponsible and inhuman robbers, manufacturers of cannon, liqueurs, and other "cultural" values. The anarchic exploitation of the physical energy of the working class brought on the European "fatherlands" the horrors of mass unemployment and hunger which, of course, ruin the health of the working people —the health of the "nation." Here is one of the effects of unemployment: on one day, August 10, the fire department in Berlin was called up fifteen times to aid people who had taken gas in an attempt to commit suicide. This figure, however, does not include those who committed suicide by drowning or hanging themselves, by using a revolver or by jumping from windows. The general cause of all these suicides was unemployment.

"That is not so much for Berlin," says one of the intellectuals who had been duped by capitalism, who realises that his master is stupid, vulgar, inhuman; but since the latter is a "man of means" one has to work for him. The duped intellectual lacks courage to work against him, on the side of the foremost international party of the working class, although he must see that history has already confronted him with the grim question of whether he has a right to be a dupe.

In almost all bourgeois countries there is a law—I do not remember its exact wording, but the sense of it is this: that if a man witnesses the committing of a crime and does not come to the assistance of the victim, he is considered an accomplice. I understand that in our days it is naïve to speak about law in capitalist society; however, I think that when the victim of the crime happens to be a bourgeois, then the bourgeoisie recognises this law.

But it is obvious that it has never been applied in cases of crimes committed against workers, against the working people. Everywhere the working class—the object and victim of the criminal deeds of the capitalists—is to-day raising its head, is beginning to feel that it should have the right to pass laws and deal out justice. Of course, it will remember the astonishing indifference of the onlookers of the cynical lawlessness perpetrated by the capitalists. When the time will come it will remember that, when the unemployed were perishing of hunger, wheat and coffee were mixed with tar to be made into bricks and used as fuel. It will remember that British fascists hired themselves out as volunteers to the armies of Bolivia and Paraguay, and that the Bolivian Consul in London calculated on purchasing the services of ten thousand of these hired murderers. The working class, the judge of all judges, will recall many things which are disregarded by those who have allowed themselves to serve as the dupes of capitalism and are not disgusted with their lives in the midst of the chaos of incredible crimes.

Who are these people and what do they think of themselves? I think that a fairly correct characterisation of them was given by the hero of a contemporary English novel, who says:

It seems to me that life demands so much attention, so much strenuous care in order to live decently, that it is hardly worth living at all. I am referring, of course, to our so-called civilised life and not to life in the Fiji Islands or in Zululand. In our life everything is so measured, foreordained, recognized, and requires so much painstaking and caution, that we never simply live, and are never at ease; not to speak of the joy of living which is denied us. We are walking a tight rope all the time, and are happy

179

only when we can tell ourselves: "Well, this section is safely behind!" If you have made up your mind to think of nothing and hunt for pleasure, you soon become surfeited and lose interest in everything; but if you try to avoid surfeit, this requires so much effort on your part, that you are no longer in a condition to enjoy life. If you swim with the current you head for catastrophe, and if you try to steer your bark you have to work hard all the time. The trouble is, you can't trust life; you have to watch it all the time, mend and darn it. Thus the only joy it can give us is like the pleasure some people derive from fussing with a radio or gramophone. So long as you change your wave-lengths and turn the dials the radio works; but that is all. You can't simply fold your hands and enjoy the music.*

Here is your aim in life: to fold your hands and look on indifferently while the storms and hurricanes of life are raging, without taking any part in it. Of course, not all European intellectuals have come to this degree of consciousness of their impotence, not all of them have come to this cold despair. But significantly it is precisely in England that this cheerless consciousness of spiritual poverty has made its appearance—in the England of Kipling, the poet of imperialism.

Having noted this fact, and also that this mood is spreading like mildew and rot all over Europe, and that it has affected lowbrow North America as well, we shall now return to the "soldierly" ideas. It has been said above that soldiers have no "soldierly" ideas, and I think that the time has passed when these ideas could be driven like nails deep into the heads of

* Retranslated from the Russian.—*Trans.*

the soldiers of the European armies. But soldierly ideas unquestionably *exist*, and to-day they are insistently propagandised in the form of fascism. These ideas are not new, their source can be traced to the books of some German writers, as, for instance, the famous historian, Heinrich Treitschke; and the philosophical artistic form of these ideas was provided by Friedrich Nietzsche in the shape of his "blond beast." Benito Mussolini is a vehicle of these ideals. In an article which he has written for the Italian Encyclopaedia he uses all the propositions of the deranged Nietzsche, his preaching of the "love for the distant," and speaks with contempt of the idea of the brotherhood of nations and the social equality of human individuals and, of course, the right of the majority to exercise authority.

Mussolini hails imperialism, under the yoke of which millions of people are perishing, and extols war as the highest expression of all human abilities—in which he was preceded by the "Futurist" Marinetti, who shouted the same idea, a maniacal idea with all military writers. In their opinion, war "ennobles" peoples; however, those who are defeated in war will hardly agree with this. Nobody has ever heard the defeated say to the victor with enthusiasm or admiration: "Oh, how nobly you have maimed and robbed me!" In 1914-15 the Belgians and French said not a word about the "nobleness" of the German victors; on the contrary, they cried out against the "ferocious Teutons" and ascribed to them brutal bloodthirstiness and other qualities that are in sharp contrast to the conception of "nobleness." Neither did the defeated and despoiled Germans say anything about the nobleness and magnanimity of the victors.

It would be very original to describe as noble such actions of the interventionists in Russia as the shooting of twenty-six

Baku Commissars by the British troops; the stealing of the gold reserve by the Czechs in Kazan; the exploit of the French and Greeks who, on the day of their evacuation from Kherson, burnt two thousand peaceful citizens, whom they had locked up in warehouses on the quay. Neither has General Graves, commander of an expeditionary force of the American interventionists in Siberia, a word to say about the "nobleness" of warriors and military. We may also mention the plundering of the Ukraine by the Germans, and we could recall many more things which have brought shame on "cultural" Europe.

Nor will the opinion of the military and fascists about the "nobleness" of war be shared by those hundreds of thousands of "victors" of whom the war made invalids and who are to-day beaten up and dispersed, as was the case with the bonus marchers in Washington.

Nor will the millions of defeated and victors, who to-day are deprived of the right to work and are starving, agree with the fascists. Italian fascism dreams of a Roman world empire; Hitler preaches that fascism will "elevate Germany above all mankind"; in Japan there is a man who asserts that soon the whole white race will be dominated by the yellow bourgeoisie; the French imperialists would like to put all of Europe in their pocket—and there are no words with which to express how beggarly hideous, how senseless and disgusting it all is. Mussolini maintains that peoples have never thirsted so passionately for strong rule.

It is very possible that here and there the bourgeoisie may yet succeed in placing on the throne fools with tilted crowns and with leaden brains under their skulls. But, of course, it will not be for long. It is all the convulsions of a moribund class that has become savage; it is all the ravings and agony of the mortally sick. Literary artists, in depicting the dying, frequently make them remember the past, pictures of their childhood and youth. It is precisely this past that the sick bourgeoisie of the whole world now sees in its ravings; and the European bourgeoisie recalls how it was at the end of the eighteenth century, when it fought under the slogan of liberty, equality, fraternity; and apparently it recalls this struggle as a sad mistake of its youth. Ah, but if it were possible to revert to feudalism! This is what the main "soldierly" ideas of fascism reduce themselves to.

In its absolutely naked form the present mood of the bourgeoisie was expressed recently with the naïve cynicism of a savage in Hitler's newspaper, *Voelkischer Beobachter,* by a certain Alfred Rosenberg, in connection with the sentence passed in Beuthen upon five fascists who tortured a Communist to death. The murder was so sadistic and disgusting that even the bourgeois court sentenced the murderers to death. Whereupon Rosenberg declared:

The sentence has revealed the deep abyss between our way of thinking and liberalism. The ruling liberal law asserts: man is equal to man. This is recognised in America too. Yet there is an impassable barrier there between whites and coloured people. Not only has the coloured man no right to marry a white woman, but he is even deprived of the right to travel in the same car with the whites. A Negro who rapes a white woman is lynched. Of course, it is "not nice," but it is necessary for the preservation of the white race. In the beginning of the war the French pacifist Jaures was assassinated, and the court pronounced the assassin not guilty; but the man who made

183

an attempt on Clemenceau's life was executed. In both cases France acted in accordance with her vital interests. Five men have been sentenced to death for killing a Pole and a Bolshevik to boot. The sentence contradicts the elementary sense of the nation's self-defence. Our offensive has been launched against the world outlook of the liberals just as against the Marxists. To us one soul is not like another, one man is not the equal of the other. Our aim is a strong German man. Only the profession of inequality gives Germany political freedom.

Under the influence of such ravings as these the sentence of the court against the murderers was mitigated and, I think, it is intended to reverse the sentence altogether. It is these ravings that represent the main content of fascism. It is quite clear that Europe and its toiling people are ruled by people who have lost their senses, that there is not a crime of which they are incapable, and that there is no measure to the amount of blood they are ready to spill. In order to come to these ravings they had to "outlive," or discard, Goethe and Kant, Schiller and Fichte, and another hundred or more of the greatest thinkers, poets, composers, and artists. The culture of the bourgeoisie remains inviolable in the privacy of the libraries and museums; exactly—inviolable in privacy. But the mode of life of the bourgeoisie is becoming ever more foul and savage, and its politics ever more sadistically inhuman. Outside the Soviet Union, it is madmen who rule the world.

1932

SOVIET INTELLECTUALS

IN the Soviet Union scientifically organised reason has received unlimited scope for its struggle against the elemental forces of nature. Vanquishing these forces and compelling them submissively to serve the great world cause of creating a classless society, reason is ever more audaciously and successfully displaying its power as a creator and organiser of a "second nature," that is, of culture, on the basis and with the forces and treasures of the first, the ancient nature which is disorganised and even hostile to the interests of labouring humanity.

Combined with the will power of the ruler, the proletariat, reason is draining swamps and extracting fuel from them, it is irrigating the arid steppe by diverting the courses of rivers, it is compelling the energy of falling water to produce electricity and fire, it is cutting roads through impassable mountains, it is vanquishing the eternal ice of the Arctic, it is joining seas by canals, it is altering the physical geography of the huge country of the Socialist Republics and making nature more fertile, wealthy, and convenient to man. New crops are being boldly introduced into the agricultural practice of our country, technical equipment is growing richer and more varied; and what is most important, children are growing up for whom our pre-revolutionary past, with all its filthy and vile abominations, will be known only from books as a mournful, fantastic, and absurd fable.

Young men will think it ridiculous if I, an old man, were to confess that I am now writing in the spirit which, in the early dawn of culture, gave rise to undying poems and legends. Yes, it is in just such a spirit that I am writing, and it is painful for me to confess that I do not command words equal to the facts that arouse my joy and pride at the admirable labour achievements of the proletariat—the dictator. My joy and pride were aroused by the opening of the White Sea and Baltic Canal. I will not speak of its economic importance to our country—that is not my field. I will deal with its social significance.

Tens of thousands of people working on the construction of the canal were hostile to the proletariat as a class, were ingrained property-lovers, people who were socially dangerous and had violated the laws of our country. But in reward for their heroic and self-sacrificing work, thousands of these people had their sentences reduced, many were altogether restored to citizenship, many were awarded premiums, and so on. Thousands were trained to become highly skilled workers. A huge force of expert hydro-technicians and builders was created, who have now gone to work on the construction of the Moscow-Volga Canal and other works of a similar nature. Having acquired more experience as builders, they will work on the construction of the Caspian-Black Sea Canal. It can be said without exaggeration that tens of thousands of people have been reformed. That is something to rejoice over, is it not?

But beyond this, there is something even more significant. This work of state and this "vitiated" human material have revealed as clearly as possible that our great and bold undertakings, which direct the physical energies of the masses into the struggle against nature, make it very easy for people to realise that it is their true mission to master the forces of nature and to subjugate their fury. I particularly insist on this thought, for I am convinced that it is worthy of attention. People who had been mutilated by the conditions of a class state—where, as is clearly shown in Europe to-day, "men are wolves to each other"—people whose energy had been directed into "socially-dangerous" channels and had found expression in acts of hostility to society, were placed in conditions in which the wolfish struggle for the most appetising scrap of bread was no longer necessary. They were given the widest opportunities for the development of their capacities; a natural and fruitful spirit of competition was awakened in them. Wreckers, kulaks, and thieves came to understand in various degrees that it was possible to live without seizing each other by the throat, that a way of life was possible in which men would not be enemies to each other, but comrades in work.

Their enemy was the unorganised and elementary power of swift rivers, granite rock, and the yielding surface of swamps. This was an enemy that could be vanquished only by the organised energy of the human collective effort. And these people became convinced of the creative power of collective labour, a power that vanquishes all obstacles. In harnessing rivers, as horses are harnessed, to work for man, many of these "enemies of society" came to realise that they were working for the enrichment and happiness of a family of one hundred and sixty million people. A literary man may well imagine that some of these former enemies began to feel themselves masters of the immeasurable forces and treasures of the earth, rather than the small property-lovers and marauders they had been. This is a feeling that makes one bigger and greater than all the heroes of all nations and ages.

That is romanticism, you say? Scarcely, comrades. I think that it is socialist realism—the realism of people who are changing and refashioning the world, the realistic metaphor that is based upon socialist experience.

Individual examples are not very convincing. Nevertheless, I feel entitled to remind you that I personally have directly experienced the saving and ennobling joy of physical labour, although a senseless and arduous labour performed for the benefit of parasites, murderers of joy, labour, and recreation, murderers of all happiness in life. To work well is to live well. This clear and simple truth is perfectly understood by thousands and hundreds of thousands of our comrades—the first builders of socialism in the world. It is a truth that firmly binds together theory and practice, ethics and aesthetics; and it should form the basis of the education of our children. Nowhere in the world are there fathers who are so fully entitled to boast to their children of the grandeur of their work as the proletariat, the dictator in the Soviet Union.

The fundamental difference between the capitalist world and ours is that our guiding idea and our whole economic practice resolutely renounce the exploitation of man by man and ceaselessly and successfully train men to be rational exploiters of the powers of nature.

Capitalism lives by the exploitation of man; it exploits the forces of nature only to the extent that these forces permit the marauding bipeds to exploit the worker as a producer and consumer, the spineless intellectual humanist as the conciliator in the inevitable struggle of classes, and the parasitic petty bourgeoisie as its reserve. And, in general, capitalism regards man as a being condemned to satisfy the idiocy of its lust for profits, and to consolidate and justify the insensate power of gold— which Vladimir Lenin said would one day be used for the building of public lavatories.

Soviet Intellectuals

I repeat what has been said many times before, namely, that nowhere in the past, even in the epochs of the greatest exertion of energy, during the Renaissance for instance, has the number of talented people increased with such rapidity and in such abundance as in our country since the October Revolution. Our talented people are chiefly inspired by the audacious desire to alter all the conditions of life from their very foundations and to build a new world. We know this as a word or phrase, but we know it very badly as expressed in actual practice, for we have no journal that would clearly and consistently give us precise summaries of our achievements in all spheres of industry, technology, science, invention, the development of agriculture, and the growing power of the mass mind. Our achievements are most successfully and strikingly expressed in science and technology. My admiration of men of science and technology has always evoked sneers, and there are some who still continue to indulge in this, inoffensive to me but, objectively, socially harmful, pastime for ignoramuses. These sneers conceal a wretched survival of the old order—an ignorant, philistine scepticism.

But there is nothing in modern times so edifying as the picture of the intellectual growth of masses and individuals in the Soviet Union. This picture compels me to look upon our scientific and technical workers as genuine heroes of our day. I am not only referring to the profound cultural-revolutionary value of their work in its various forms—this is not the place to speak of that. But I would like to say a few words about our scientist and our engineer as a social type.

He is a man of a new type. He is new, not only because he has resolutely rejected the precept "science for science's sake" professed by the scientific experts of the bourgeoisie, the pre-

189

cept of the searchers after "lasting truth"—our young scientist knows that there are no eternal truths and that every truth is nothing but an implement of knowledge, a step forward and upward. He is a new type of man because he differs from all other masters of culture in the fact that he is taking a direct part in the practical work of changing the world, that he is an indicator of the latent, "potential" talent of the working people. And one of his most valuable features is a feeling of responsibility—a truly socialist feeling, in my opinion. He feels his responsibility to the material with which he works, to the technical process in which he participates, to the collective body in whose midst he displays his capacity, to the party and class of which he is not a hireling, but one of the creative units. He is part of a working collective body, a necessary, and sometimes the chief part; he unites and concentrates the energy of the collective body in the process of labour. He cannot help feeling the deep meaning of his responsibility.

One involuntarily and not without a certain sadness compares the engineer and scientific worker with some of our other masters and conveyors of culture to the masses, as, for example, the actor and writer. The actor and writer are better known to society; they enjoy the attention, sympathy, and solicitude of society and the government far more than scientific and technical workers do. The labour of the masters of technology and science—not to mention the labour of the doctor, the sentinel and champion of the health of the people, or the labour of the teacher, who opens the eyes of children to the world surrounding them—is not yet as well paid as the labour of famous writers.

There are very serious grounds for asserting that the sense of social responsibility is far less developed among literary men than among other masters of culture. One might even ask: Does the writer recognise his responsibility to the reader, to the epoch, and to society, or does he feel responsible only to the critics? One very often observes a poor sense of responsibility in our literary men, or even no sense of responsibility at all, to the material they handle. The degree of individualism is much higher among literary men than among other masters of culture. It is said that this is due to the nature of their work. I do not undertake to judge. The individualism of the engineer and the scientist is determined by their speciality; the astronomer or astro-physicist need not necessarily be acquainted with geology or medicine, and a builder of locomotives or bridges probably need not be acquainted with ethnography and zoology.

But the writer should know, if not everything, at least as much as possible about the astronomer and the mechanic, the biologist and the tailor, the engineer and the shepherd, and so on. It is not enough to say of the bug that it is red or brown, which is what our writers usually say of the enemies of the proletariat. Our writers have a good knowledge and understanding of certain ancient aphorisms, such as: "Thou art a tsar; live thine own life." This wretched little aphorism is a false one. The tsars used to surround themselves with a vast host of servitors. And, in imitation of the tsars, literary barons also try to surround themselves with a retinue. The writers have not deleted another old aphorism from their lexicon: "Art for art's sake"—and some of the smart ones are trying to fabricate a refined literature, in imitation, for example, of Dos Passos. They are still disputing over the alleged contradiction between form and content, as though form is possible without content. For instance, a gun made of air—although air is also

191

a material—is not a gun that can fire real shells. The more important the social significance of the material, the stricter, more precise, and clearer a form it demands. It seems to me high time this were understood.

There are quite a number of writers who are unconcerned about making the productions of their minds and pens at least relatively comprehensible to their readers. I have repeatedly raised this point before, but in vain. If you say even to a not very competent writer,—"Comrade, what you have written is not very good!", he gets annoyed, runs off to complain—and soon an article appears claiming that the writer mentioned is a genius. There are some who believe that since "it was so," then "it will be so"; they very assiduously delve into the filth of the past and, finding some survivals of it in the present, claim not without satisfaction that the past resembles the present. Mutually sympathetic groups are formed which vilify groups antipathetic to them; the *Literary Gazette* answers in the same coin—and this unseemly mix-up is called "literary life." As a knowledge of truth is obtained from a comparison of "contradictions," I, of course, am not opposed to groups, provided each of them is formed under the influence of a similar experience and does not try to hector and domineer, but to compare its experience with the experiences of others, and provided it does so honestly, with the object of attaining some higher ideological unity necessary for an alliance of writers.

It will be said: "He began with a toast, and has ended with a funeral oration." It looks very much like it, but not quite. For literature is a cause—and in our country and under our conditions—a very important cause. Moreover, the force of life is such that I am ready to believe that the dead may be resurrected.

Soviet Intellectuals

Dear comrades, you are living in an atmosphere in which the collective labour of the masses is altering the physical geography of the earth; an atmosphere in which an unprecedented and amazingly audacious and successful struggle with nature has begun; an atmosphere which is re-educating wreckers, enemies of the proletariat, ingrained property-lovers, "socially dangerous" people, and making them useful and active citizens. Is it not time perhaps, comrades, for you, too, to re-educate yourselves and become genuine masters of your craft and active collaborators of the proletariat, which is working for the freedom and the happiness of the proletariat of all countries?

There is such a thing as a hummock view and a point of view. The distinction should be observed. We know that hummocks are a peculiarity of swamps, and that they are left after the swamp has been drained. Not much can be seen from a hummock. A point of view is different; it is formed as a result of a writer's observation, comparison, and study of the diverse phenomena of life. The broader the social experience of the writer, the more elevated is his point of view, the broader is his intellectual horizon, and the clearer can he see what is concerned with what and the reciprocal action of approaches and contacts on earth. Scientific socialism has created for us an elevated intellectual plateau, from which the past can be clearly observed and from which the only path into the future is visible, the path leading from "the realm of necessity to the realm of freedom." The successful progress of the work of the Party created by the political genius of Vladimir Lenin is convincing the proletariat of all countries, and even men of sense who are hostile to the proletariat as a class, that the path from "the realm of necessity to the realm of freedom" is not a fantasy. The death agony of the bourgeoisie known as fascism, and especially the frightful agony of the German bourgeoisie, shows even more convincingly that the path of the proletariat is the right one. The iron will of Joseph Stalin, the helmsman of the Party, is splendidly coping with deviations from the proper course and curing the crew of the Party vessel of all attacks of "dizziness." To this it should be added that history is ever more resolutely and effectively working for us.

This is optimism, you say? No. We must clearly perceive all the vileness and despicableness that is threatening us from abroad, that is threatening the first state in the history of mankind to be built by a proletarian dictatorship on the principles of scientific socialism. We must ruthlessly and mercilessly combat everything that is hostile to the fundamental aim of the proletariat and capable of retarding its cultural-revolutionary, socialist growth. And we must firmly realise that although in certain countries the movement of the proletariat towards power is being retarded, nevertheless there is no force that can halt it. Our system of political education of the masses teaches the truth, to which capitalism can retaliate only by force of arms; but the arms are in the hands of the proletariat. The shameful civic death of the "leaders" of the German Social-Democracy was the suicide of cowards terrified by the spread of revolutionary truth.

It is vitally essential for the creative work of our writers that they acquire the point of view from which—and from which alone—can be clearly seen all the filthy crimes of capitalism, all the vileness of its bloody intentions, and all the grandeur of the heroic work of the proletarian dictatorship. One can rise to this point of view only by ridding oneself of the professional, craft mesh, the mesh of commonplace in which we are slowly being entangled, perhaps without ourselves observing it. We must understand that by succumbing to the life of the commonplace, we run the risk of becoming parasites on the working class, public clowns, as the majority of the writers of the bourgeoisie have always been.

The anxiety which induces me to speak in this way is not peculiar to me; it is felt by Nikolai Tikhonov, one of our most talented writers, the author of the article "The Indifferent," and one senses it in friendly conversations with the more responsive of our young writers, those who are sincerely and eagerly concerned about the fate of literature and who understand its cultural and educational value. Anxiety is also caused by the indifference shown by writers to the organisation of their own all-Union congress. One asks: What will the literary men of the centre have to offer the hundreds of young writers from the regions and republics? What will they say to these young people? It is to be expected that the former members of the RAPP * will once again repent their errors in public, and that, despite their repentance, their former enemies, friends, and colleagues will once again subject them to severe criticism, the sort of criticism that can teach nothing but is quite capable of increasing the irresponsibility of certain writers.

The other day the members of the Organising Committee were asked what they had done by way of preparation for the all-Union congress. They could not give a coherent answer, although the enquiry concerned a matter of "vital" interest to them.

The ability with which they pronounced lengthy and vague speeches revealed the anemia of their minds. Some of them demonstratively strolled past the groups engaged in conversa-

* Russian Association of Proletarian Writers.—*Trans.*

tion, seemingly admiring the wretched weather, and apparently convinced that geniuses they were and geniuses they would remain under all conditions. Not one of them regretted that he had not found time to visit the work on the White Sea and Baltic Canal; not one of them was acquainted with the results of the two years' work done by Angelo Omedo, one of the greatest hydrographers and hydro-electric engineers living, in Transcaucasia, the Caucasus, Central Asia, and Siberia; not one of them was interested in the state of the huge project for an Institute of Experimental Medicine; and, in general, the progress of the new culture is something that apparently lies beyond their field of vision, and that whatever knowledge they may have of it is derived solely from newspapers—not very nourishing pabulum for literary artists. For example, just now huts are being built outside Moscow for thousands of workers engaged in the construction of the Volga-Moscow Canal. These thousands of people of various types constitute splendid study material. I am not certain that any of my "colleagues of the pen" will devote the slightest attention to this rich material.

I have not forgotten that during these fifteen years our young literature has produced scores of very valuable books. But I have also not forgotten that the number of themes dealt with in these books is by no means very large, and that many of the themes, treated hastily and superficially, have been compromised, that is, spoilt.

One cannot help noting the fact that, with the exception of M. Ognyev and a few others, our writers have not produced a single valuable book on children—for fathers and mothers—not to speak of books for children, which are evidently considered to be unworthy of "high art." Nobody has dealt with the theme of the regeneration of the peasant in the factory, or of the

196

intellectual and emotional transformation of members of the national minorities into Communist internationalists, we have not had a clear portrait of the woman-administrator, nobody has given us portraits of the scientific worker, the inventor, the artist—portraits of people many of whom were born in remote villages or in the filthy back-streets of the cities, or brought up in chimneyless huts together with the calves, or on city outskirts together with beggars and thieves. Yet many of them are already known to Europe as people of the highest talent. But in our own country they are unknown—or else have been forgotten.

Very narrow indeed is the outlook of our literary comrades; and the cause of this narrowness is—the hummock view. Millions and tens of millions of proletarians in all parts of the world are expecting ardent and vivid productions from us; they are expecting clear and simple descriptions of the great achievements of masses and individuals in which the miraculous energy of the masses is concentrated. However much the world bourgeois press may slander us, however assiduously it may invent abominable falsehoods about us, however diehard parliamentarians may lie and try to discredit our work, even this press is obliged to admit the success of our diplomacy. And the European proletariat, territorially situated closest to us, is hearing more and more frequently from the mouth of his enemy, the bourgeoisie, acknowledgements of the great achievements of "socialism in one country."

The writers of the Union of Soviet Socialist Republics must broaden their outlook in order to broaden and deepen their activities. This is demanded of them by the epoch, by the new history which the proletariat of the Soviet Union is creating; it is demanded by the children who will soon become adolescents and may put some rather disconcerting questions to their fathers; and, lastly, it is demanded by art.

The foreign and internal enemies will no doubt rejoice and say: "Here is Gorky, too, giving us some enjoyable spiritual food!" But their rejoicing will be misguided. I have no intention of feeding pigs. This article has been called forth by the great demands of real life in the Soviet Union. The enemies are constitutionally incapable of realising the greatness and value of these demands. The literature of the Soviet Union is developing well, but real life is splendid and magnificent. Literature must attain to the level of real life. That is the point.

1933

HUMANISM AND CULTURE

THE writers' congress in Paris was organised under the slogan of the defence of culture against the destructive onslaughts of fascism. It was apparently assumed that the real, factual content of the concept, the "culture" of the contemporary bourgeoisie, was defined identically by all the members of the congress, and that there could be no divergence of opinion as to its interpretation. But was this the case?

Fascism is the offspring, the cancerous tumor of bourgeois culture which is now advanced to the stage of putrefaction and dissolution. The theoreticians and practitioners of fascism are adventurers drawn by the bourgeoisie from its own midst. In Italy, in Germany the bourgeoisie handed over the political, physical power to the fascists, whom it controls with almost the same Machiavellian cunning with which the medieval bourgeoisie of the Italian towns controlled the *condottieri*. Not only does it observe with satisfaction and encourage the most abominable slaughter of proletarians by the fascists, but it permits them to persecute and exile from their fatherland writers and scientists, *i.e.*, the representatives of its own intellectual strength, which it but recently flaunted and boasted of.

Satisfying the aspirations of its imperialist masters for a new redivision of the world through a new world slaughter, fascism came forth with the theory of the right of the German race to rule throughout the world and over all races. This long-forgotten idea of the sick Friedrich Nietzsche concerning the priority of the "blond beast" had its origin in the fact of the subjugation of Hindus, Indo-Chinese, Melanesians, and Polynesians, Negroes, etc. by the fair-haired race. This idea flourished in the years when the German bourgeoisie, having defeated its Austrian and French rivals, wished to participate in the colonial pillage along with the British, Dutch, and French bourgeoisie. This theory of the right of the white race to rule the world permits each national group of the bourgeoisie to consider not only the coloured races but also its white European neighbours as barbarians to be enslaved or destroyed. This theory which the Italian and Japanese bourgeoisie have already put into practice is one of the real facts which enter into the contemporary concept, "culture."

The voices of the bourgeois dignitaries of Europe grow ever louder; they cry about the overproduction of intellectuals, about the necessity of curtailing education and putting a "brake" on the development of culture; even about the superfluity of technique, about a return to hand labour. The archbishop of York, speaking at the opening of a school at Bournemouth, declared:

> I should like to see a stop put to all invention. If I could destroy the internal combustion engine I should certainly do so.

His colleague of the same compromised profession, the archbishop of Canterbury, apparently admits the necessity of technique, for he preaches a "crusade" against the Soviet Union— and the new war, according to experts, will be a "war of machines." If the utterances of London and Roman vicars of Christ on earth, as well as of all the other bourgeois preachers who advocate putting an end to the growth of culture—men who have obviously lost their minds from hate of the proletariat or from fear of the inevitable social catastrophe—if these utterances had been made, say, in the 'eighties of the nineteenth century, they would have been regarded by the bourgeoisie as an expression of idiocy, a summons to barbarism.

In our time, when the bourgeoisie has become completely blind to the difference between courage and shamelessness, an appeal for a return to the Middle Ages is dubbed "courageous thought."

Thus we see that European bourgeois culture is not the "monolithic whole" that bourgeois historians picture. Its "living force" has split up into profiteers and bankers who, regarding all other men as a cheap and plentiful commodity, wish to hold on at any cost to their elevated, socially comfortable positions; into men who defend their right to work for the further development of culture; and into fascists who, it may be, are also men, but who, as a result of a prolonged intoxication, spread over a number of generations, have grown anti-social, and who require strict isolation, or even more decisive measures to put an end to their abominable, bloody crimes.

The journalists of the chief Parisian papers, almost ignoring the question of the fascist menace to bourgeois culture, set forth the fundamental question of the epoch. The newspaper *Vandemiere* asks:

> The French organizers of the Congress for the Defence of Culture are five revolutionary writers: Barbusse, Jean Richard Bloch, André Gide, André Malraux, and Romain Rolland. Do these names not arouse a certain distrust?
> When we see such names as those we have cited, we

201

have the right to ask: What culture do they invite us to defend?

The question is perfectly relevant and properly put. Five or six such papers as *Figaro, Temps, Echo de Paris,* etc., in differently constructed phrases put the question of the epoch still more sharply. They ask: Can Communism be the heir to Western-European culture, which is based on Greek and Roman cultural values?

The question is put with extreme clarity like a challenge to a verbal combat. In order that a dispute may be productive, it is first necessary to determine what we are disputing about, what we reject and deny, what we defend and affirm. What real, factual content do the defenders of contemporary bourgeois culture attribute to this concept, the meaning of which has long been unclear—"culture?"

A certain Maurice Bourdet assumes that it is necessary and possible to "define and confine the limits of culture," that its fundamental creative sources are labour—the physical source and technology—and the intellectual source. The writer of these lines is inclined to think that any ideology is, essentially, and in the broad sense of the term, a technology—a system of working and logical methods by means of which mankind widens its knowledge of the world in order gradually to change the world. We see that the bourgeoisie of our day is quite content with what it has; that it actually and very successfully "sets limits to the normal growth of culture," creating many millions of unemployed, agitating for a decrease in the use of technique, curtailing funds for the upkeep of higher schools, museums, etc. It is well known that the only branch of industry which works uninterruptedly and is continually expanding is the war industry, intended for the destruction of millions of workers and peasants on the fields of future battles, where the Western-European bourgeoisie plans to settle its international controversy as to which of its national groups should dominate over the others.

The captains of the coming blood-bath, organised by the bourgeoisie in order to profit by the blood of their enslaved neighbours, loudly and coldbloodedly declare that this war will be still more destructive and ruinous than that of 1914-18. Here it is proper to recall some facts of the last war, the losses and ruins of which have already been effaced by the toil of the proletariat and the peasantry, *i.e.*, the classes which suffered most from the mad frenzy of the bourgeoisie.

The facts are as follows. By 1915 Germany was experiencing a shortage of lubricating oils. The matter came to the point where the Germans were paying in Copenhagen 1,800 marks for a keg of oil which cost at that time no more than 200 marks. The American ambassador in Berlin wrote, in December of that year, to his government: "The lack of lubricating oil will soon bring about Germany's defeat." At the same time British freighters were bringing to Copenhagen kegs of the indispensable oils. This fact is confirmed by the statistics of the British Ministry of Trade. Germany would have experienced a shortage of coal at the beginning of 1915 had she not been supplied with English coal through the Scandinavian countries. Thus, for example, in the month of September, 1914, Sweden received 33,000 tons of coal, almost all of which was despatched to the central powers.

Only thanks to this monstrous liberality of England was Ludendorff able, in June, 1917, to refuse to withdraw 50,000 men from the army for work in the Ruhr mines.

Culture and the People

The export of coal to Sweden soon attained the enormous figure of 100,000 and even 150,000 tons a month, that is, twice the pre-war yearly consumption of coal of these countries. The British ambassador to Copenhagen, Sir Wolf Paget, testified that this coal went for the slaughter of English soldiers, but his voice went unheard.

It has been ascertained that during the war the French capitalists provided their enemies, the German capitalists, with nickel or zinc and that an English munitions manufacturer exchanged certain destructive inventions with a German armaments manufacturer. Many more such facts, no less vile and criminal, have so far not been ascertained, *i.e.*, have not been "made public," have not been published. Thus we see that war does not interfere with trade, and that it was only a matter of "a friendly quarrel" over the blood and corpses of millions of proletarians. The proletariat, unfortunately, does not as yet understand that it ought not to wipe out and mutilate its class brothers, that after the war it will be forced to clear up at a miserable wage all the wreckage, to repair all the damages sustained by the capitalists.

Simple, clear, truly humanitarian justice tells us that the product of labour should belong to him who made it, and not to him who ordered it to be made. Weapons—any weapons— are the product of the workers' labour.

So we now have some idea of the real factual content of the concept: Western-European "culture of the modern bourgeoisie, based upon Greek and Roman values." Here it is proper to add something from the field of "international morals," something effected recently by the British bourgeoisie. This insular bourgeoisie long ago won from its neighbours the epithet "treacherous," that is, shameless, hypocritical, Jesuitical. As is well known, the British gave the French bourgeoisie certain solemn promises, the gist of which was that they would defend the French capitalists in case of a war with the German capitalists. It was even said that "the frontiers of England are on the Rhine," that is, on the French-German frontier. The phrase about frontiers proved ambiguous, inasmuch as the British bourgeois came to an understanding with the German, thus violating their promises. Possibly the frontiers of England will prove to be on the Rhine, but not in order to defend the French, but only after the latter have been crushed by an Anglo-German alliance. All is possible among people who possess "neither honour nor conscience."

The French journalists put this question: "Will a culture of such antiquity, a culture which is the heir of the Greek and Roman cultural values, continue its mission, in spite of all obstacles, or must it give way to a new form of culture, which intends to proclaim the dominance of economics over the spirit?"

When Messieurs the Journalists speak of "the dominance of economics over the spirit," they thoughtlessly and mechanically give expression to their ignorance or—and this is more likely—to their brazenness. Of course, it is possible that some of them have not as yet shed the naïve illusion of "spiritual" independence, although they are completely dependent upon their editors, who are body and soul dependent upon the publishers —bankers, lords, manufacturers of armaments.

Let the naïve journalists—if such exist—honestly and carefully look about them, and they shall see that the "economics" of two-legged spiders, expressed in the coarsest materialist forms, dominates precisely in the capitalist states, while the "new form of culture" sets itself the aim of freeing toiling humanity from the violence of the now meaningless economics created by the "spirit" of Sir Basil Zaharoff, Deterding, Vickers, Creusot, Hearst, Schneider, Kreuger, Stavitsky, and the other true leaders of contemporary bourgeois culture. It is ridiculous to dream about, still more to speak about individual independence in a society where people—and among them the journalists—are sold and bought as easily and "freely" as sheep or cucumbers.

To what extent the poison has entered the rotting spirit of bourgeois culture is revealed with impressive force by the grandiose scale of the swindling and the paltriness of the swindlers themselves. This paltriness clearly testifies to the exhaustion of the specific talents of the European bourgeois, to the "degeneration of the type." John Law was a genius in comparison with Stavitsky, or "the match king" Ivan Kreuger.

The vicious, decaying "spirit" of the contemporary bourgeoisie is vividly expressed in the quantitative increase of traitors and the qualitative rise in their loathsomeness. Until the 'twenties of the twentieth century Europe hardly knew such traitors as Noske, the self-designated "blood-hound," his colleagues Ebert and Haase and, in general, the leaders of the Second International. A picture of the life of the bourgeoisie— a cross section of it as it is phlegmatically drawn from day to day by the journalists of Europe—is repellent, terrible. It is altogether understandable that their routine professional work amidst blood and filth deadens all sensitivity of feeling, arouses in the journalists no desire to draw conclusions from their observations. Indifferently "recording facts," they colour them still more grandly with blood and filth for the diversion of the bourgeoisie reader; and he, nourished on descriptions of crime, becomes still more arrogant and stupid. It is well known that the most popular literature of the middle and petty bourgeoisie is the detective story.

I may be permitted to ask: Where and in what forms have the "Greek and Latin cultural values" been preserved amidst this filth and decay? As "material" values they are preserved in museums, in the collections of millionaires, inaccessible to the toiling masses and to the petty bourgeoisie. As "spiritual" values, for example, the works of Aeschylus, Sophocles, Euripides should be produced in the theatres, but in Europe this is not done. In bourgeois universities, professors lecture on Roman law, on ancient Greek philosophy, and other values, including international law and even medieval humanism. We leave it to the journalists of Europe to discover where these values are to be found in the chaos of contemporary life and to indicate their practical, educational significance. It seems to us that if contemporary Europe recalls ancient Rome, it is the Rome of decline and collapse.

The bourgeois intellectuals play an extremely strange and pathetic *rôle* in the process of decay and disintegration of the ruling class of contemporary Europe. They of course know where their bread is buttered, and in defending a "culture" which has outlived its day, the intellectuals defend the power of their own class. This power has always been served technologically as well as ideologically by more or less highly qualified intellectuals and this is true also at the present time. In 1914 the European bourgeoisie sent thousands of such intellectuals to the front as rank and file soldiers and forced them to kill each other. Before they were maimed, gassed, or killed, these "masters of culture" actively participated in the destruction of cities, in the devastation of the fertile soil and in other acts of the destruction of culture.

Culture and the People

Most of these intellectuals were proletarians, and they ended their lives in order to strengthen the power of the property holders. Later dozens of intellectuals wrote books in which they described the madness of war and heaped curses upon it. Now the bourgeoisie is preparing a new international slaughter on a still grander scale. Since in the recent past the iron hand of war did not show the slightest respect for the illustrious mementos and depositories of cultural values, it is exceedingly probable that in the next war the British Museum, the Louvre, and the numerous museums of the ancient capitals will be turned into rubbish and dust. And thousands of bearers of intellectual energy, of "masters of culture," will be destroyed along with millions of the strongest workers and peasants. And to what purpose? To satisfy the desire of some large group of profiteers and bankers to subjugate and rob some other group. It has been repeatedly and indisputably proved that the periodical bourgeois slaughters are nothing but armed pillage, that is, a crime punishable by the bourgeois law of all lands.

The idiotic criminality of the bourgeois becomes particularly repellent when one reflects on the great amount of skilled, valuable labour, metal and inventions the shopkeepers destroyed yesterday and will destroy to-morrow. How many cities, factories, plants will be turned into dust! How many splendid ships will be sunk! How much land will be devastated! Large numbers of children will be killed. And finally, the criminal insanity of the surfeited classes results in forcing workers, peasants, and intellectuals to work for the destruction of the products of their labour and each other.

"The dominance of economics" finds complete expression in the coarse, zoological materialism of the property owners. The poisonous "spirit" of this rapacious materialism of the fat, two-legged spiders no longer troubles to cover itself with the out-worn tatters of religion and philosophy. Fascism and the racial theory are a cynical, forthright apologia of armed robbery. Such is the spirit of modern bourgeois "culture"—a loathsome, abominable spirit. We see that honest intellectuals, suffocating in such a milieu, flee from the land where to-day this spirit finds most arrogant, most thorough expression. But to-morrow—if the proletariat but permit—this spirit will manifest itself as cynically, as arrogantly in the lands where they have taken refuge.

Quite naturally the question arises: What right to power has the modern bourgeoisie, which denies the principles of its culture, which has lost all ability for management, which is creating an ever more frightful unemployment, which shamelessly despoils workers, peasants, and colonies in order to further its war preparations; what right to exist and to rule has a class which senselessly exhausts the working and creative energy of the whole world, a class quantitatively infinitesimal, qualitatively vicious and criminal? And this class holds in its bloody hands the fate of almost two billion European, Chinese, Indian, African peasants and workers. The sombre grotesqueness of this fact will be made the clearer if we compare it with another fact.

There exists a land where the will and intellect of all the workers and peasants are stimulated and developed by socially-necessary labour, equally beneficial to each working unit, and where the whole mass of labour energy is drawn into the varied work of creating new conditions of life, that is, of a new socialist culture—

where the proletariat, following the teachings of Marx and Lenin, and led by Joseph Stalin, has freed the peasantry from the idiotic "power of the soil," from a tame submission to the caprices of nature, from the pernicious influence of private property, where the proletariat has transformed the property owner into a collectivist;

where the proletarian, the hewer of wood and drawer of water of bourgeois society, has proved that when equipped with knowledge he is quite capable of becoming a master and creator of culture, where the cultural work of the individual is valued by the whole working population more highly than it has ever been valued anywhere else, and where this esteem continually aids in the growth of the individual and his work;

where women—half the country's population—are on a basis of equality with the men, heroically work shoulder to shoulder with them in all fields, where rational energy is applied, and where women's talents, daring and enthusiasm for work grow with tremendous speed;

where the children are brought up away from the corrupting influence of the church, whose aim is to instil in men patience, meekness, submission to "the powers that be";

where a multitude of various, numerically insignificant, half-savage peoples, that formerly had no written language, now possess their own literature, have been granted the right to free development and reveal to the world the primitive freshness of their reflections and sensations, their ability to work and the beautiful simplicity of their poetry;

where ancient tribes, whose culture was formerly suppressed by the colonial policy of the profiteers and the tsar, now reveal their splendid talents and the treasures of a liberated spirit.

In this land the artist and the scientist only serve the will of the working masses, a will which strives to assimilate all the cultural values of mankind.

Humanism and Culture

But this land is surrounded by enemies who envy its riches, who fear its beneficial influence upon the toilers of the whole world, and dream of a plundering onslaught upon her. Therefore the ardent desire to know the past, so indispensable for the moulding of the future, is to some extent limited by the necessity of working for the defence of the country, thereby retarding to a certain degree the growth of its material culture and enrichment. This desire to know the past is also to a certain extent restricted by the fact that in the heritage of bourgeois culture honey and poison are strongly mixed, and that the "verities" of bourgeois learning about the history of mankind possess all the wiles of an old experienced coquette pretending to be an innocent girl.

Man is dear to the proletariat. Even if a man displayed antisocial tendencies and has behaved for some time as a socially dangerous individual, he is not confined in the demoralizing inactivity of a prison, but re-educated into a skilled worker, a useful member of society. This firmly established attitude towards the "criminal" throws light upon the active humanism of the proletariat, a humanism which has never existed and cannot exist in a society where *homo homini lupus est.*

The workers' and peasants' power of the U.S.S.R. is wisely concerned with the toilers' spiritual health, and especially with the health of the children and the youth. Just as diligently and ably does it look after physical education, after the preservation of physical health. It was for this purpose that the All-Union Institute of Experimental Medicine, the first institute in the world for the all-round study of the human organism was established.

One can point out many entirely new undertakings which are rapidly and decisively enriching the land and changing its physical appearance. Industry is continually expanding, agriculture is being reorganised, new crops and fruits are being introduced, while grain and root plants are being moved ever farther north, swamps are being drained and arid regions irrigated, rivers are being united by canals; from year to year the country grows richer in electric power, its explored resources of coal, oil, metal ores, mineral fertilizers steadily increase, the Arctic is being conquered. This, of course, is not all that is being done in the country that feels a shortage of labour power at a time when the profiteers of Europe and the United States throw millions out of employment.

All that has been done in the U.S.S.R. has been done in less than two decades, and this speaks most eloquently for the ability of the peoples of the Soviet Union, for their heroic labour, for the fact that in our country labour is becoming an art, for the fact that the proletariat of the U.S.S.R., led by the teachings and Party of Lenin, and by the inexhaustible, ever-growing energy of Joseph Stalin, is creating a new culture, a new history of mankind. And what is the real, factual meaning of the concept: the "culture" of the modern bourgeoisie? At the basis of all that has been briefly and incompletely enumerated here, there operates the mighty, creative energy of proletarian humanism—the humanism of Marx and Lenin. This is not the humanism on which the bourgeoisie but recently prided themselves as the basis of their civilisation and culture.

Apart from the word "humanism," these two humanisms have nothing in common. The word is the same, but the meaning is utterly different. This humanism which appeared about five hundred years ago was a means of self-defence for the bourgeoisie against the feudal lords and the church, its "spiritual leader," which was also ruled by the feudal lords. When

Humanism and Culture

the rich bourgeois, manufacturer, or merchant spoke of the "equality" of men, he understood by this his own personal equality to the feudal parasite in knightly armour or in a bishop's vestment. Bourgeois humanism existed amiably side by side with slavery, slave trading, with the "law of the first night," with the Inquisition, with the wholesale extermination of the Albigenses in Toulouse, with the burning at the stake of Jan Hus, Giordano Bruno, and tens of thousands of nameless "heretics," "witches," artisans, peasants who were enthralled by the echoes of primitive communism preserved in the Old and New Testaments.

Did the bourgeoisie ever oppose the ferocity of the church and the feudal lords? As a class—never. The only protest came from lone individuals in its midst, and the bourgeoisie exterminated them. In the past the bourgeois humanists aided the feudal lords as assiduously in the destruction of Wat Tyler's peasant army, the French "Jacques," the "Taborites," as the cultured profiteers of the twentieth century who coldbloodedly and ferociously slaughter the workers in the streets of Vienna, Antwerp, Berlin, in Spain, in the Philippine Islands, in the cities of India, in China, everywhere. Is it necessary to speak of the abominable crimes which are well known to all, and which testify to the fact that "humanism as the basis of bourgeois culture" has to-day lost all meaning? They no longer speak of it; apparently they realise that it is too shameless to mention "humanism" while almost daily they shoot down hungry workers in the streets of the cities, pack the prisons with them, and behead or sentence to hard labour thousands of the most active of them.

In general the bourgeoisie has never tried to alleviate the life of the workers by any other means than charity, which robs the worker of his dignity. The humanism of the philistines found practical expression in "philanthropy," that is, in giving alms to the people whom they had robbed. They devised and practised a very stupid, swindling commandment: "Let not thy right hand know what thy left hand doeth." And then, having plundered billions, these "lords of life" spent miserly pence for schools, hospitals, and homes for invalids. The literature of the philistines preached "mercy" to the downfallen, but these downfallen were the same people whom the bourgeoisie had robbed, struck down, trampled in the mire.

If bourgeois humanism were genuine, if it sincerely strove to arouse and foster in the men whom it had enslaved the sense of human dignity, a consciousness of their collective strength, a consciousness of the significance of man as the organiser of the world and the forces of nature, it would not advocate the despicable idea of the inevitability of suffering, nor the passive feeling of sympathy, but it would stimulate an active hostility to all suffering, especially the suffering engendered by social economic conditions.

Physical pain is a warning by the human organism that some harmful element has entered its normal activity. In this manner the organism cries: Man, defend thyself! The humanism of the philistines, in preaching sympathy, teaches reconciliation with that frightful pain caused by the allegedly unavoidable, everlasting relations of the classes, the humiliating division of men into superior and inferior races and peoples, into white aristocrats and "coloured" slaves. This division impedes the growth of the toilers' consciousness of the unity of their interests—the very purpose for which it was established.

The humanism of the revolutionary proletariat is straightforward. It does not pronounce grandiloquent and sweet phrases of love for mankind. Its aim is to free the proletariat of the whole world from the shameful, bloody, insane yoke of capitalism, to teach men not to consider themselves as commodities which are bought and sold, to serve as the raw material for the manufacture of gold and the luxuries of the philistines. Capitalism violates the world as a senile old man violates a young, healthy woman whom he is impotent to impregnate with anything besides the diseases of senility. The task of proletarian humanism does not demand lyrical declarations of love; it demands from each worker a consciousness of his historic mission, of his right to power, a revolutionary activity which is especially necessary on the eve of a new war, which, in the last analysis, is directed by the capitalists against him.

Proletarian humanism demands an undying hate of philistinism, of the capitalist rule and its lackeys, of parasites, of the fascists and executioners, of the traitors to the working class; hatred for all that causes suffering and all who live by the sufferings of hundreds of millions of people. I believe that from this schematic summary of realistic data, the values of bourgeois and proletarian culture will be made sufficiently clear to every honest person.

1935

WE MUST KNOW THE PAST *

I AM late in answering your interesting letter, Effrosinya Ivanovna. I am also somewhat of a weaver, but my days are occupied in weaving words just as yours in weaving yarn.

The letter you wrote was splendid. Reading it one sees how the heart of woman is growing wiser, how—but recently the "all-enduring long-suffering mother of the Russian progeny"— she is now, in the Union of Soviets becoming the mistress of her land, understanding the mighty significance of free labour and the socialist system which is transforming the world. One sees this and, of course, rejoices. But what particularly gladdens one is that the women of the working class are learning to speak of their hard past; and also that books are appearing so needed by the youth as, for instance, those by Alena Novikova, Agrippina Korevanova, and Galina Grekova—who when only nine years old worked as a farm-hand for rich Kuban Cossacks and who is now teaching philosophy in the universities. We must know the past, for without this knowledge one is liable to lose one's bearings in life, and land again in that reeking, bloody mire from which the wise teachings of Vladi-

* Effrosinya Ivanovna Semyonova, a weaver in the Trekhgornaya Textile Mills, wrote a letter to the author, published in the *Komsomolskaya Pravda*, September 21, 1935. In this letter she told the great writer of the impressions his famous novel, *Mother*, had made on her. This old proletarian woman informed him that she was now striving her utmost to "stamp out my ignorance and become a still more useful person to our society." "We Must Know the Past" is his reply.—*Trans.*

216

We Must Know the Past

mir Ilyich Lenin led us and set us on the broad, straight road towards a great and happy future. He taught:

> One can become a Communist only when one enriches one's mind with the knowledge of all the wealth created by mankind. . . .

> It would be a mistake to believe that it is sufficient to learn Communist slogans, the conclusions of Communist science, and that it is not necessary to acquire the sum of knowledge of which Communism itself is a consequence. . . .

> Without work, without struggle, a book knowledge of Communism obtained from Communist books and works would be worthless, for it would continue the old separation of theory from practice, the old separation that was the most disgusting feature of the old bourgeois society.*

For us and especially for our successors, the youth, it is just as important to arm ourselves with knowledge as to arm ourselves with steel in order to beat off our enemies. We have lived to see the time when the world-wide scoundrel—the bourgeoisie—has completely lost its mind from fear of its inevitable doom and when its main force—avarice—is revealed before us in a more loathsome aspect than ever before.

The world's profiteers have become so accustomed to the impunity of their deeds and to inhumane actions that this has assumed unusually insolent scope, as we see in the case of the seizure of Manchuria, the subjugation of China, Mussolini's attempt to enslave the Abyssinians and Hitler's prepara-

* V. I. Lenin, *Selected Works*, Vol. IX (London and New York), pp. 471, 470, 469.—*Trans.*

tions for a new European slaughter. We must know that the profiteers are once again preparing for a new redivision of the world in order to attack us, our rich country, where the parasites on the working class have been destroyed, where a classless society is being built, a new life is coming into being, where a force irreconcilably hostile to the profiteers is growing and which threatens them with their doom.

We are not Manchurians and not Chinese or Abyssinians; we are already a people of socialist culture, and we are not unarmed. Our arms are not only in the hands of the men of the excellent Red Army, they are in the wise and world-saving teachings of Lenin and Stalin, they are in the magnificent work of developing and amassing the toiling and fighting energy necessary for our self-defence. The proletarians of all lands attentively watch our life and work, they are learning by our example how to fight against their executioners and plunderers. This puts us under the obligation of working and studying still more intensively, of arming ourselves still more carefully, and you, Effrosinya Ivanovna, are correct in deciding to "stamp out" your "ignorance," and make yourself a staunch, tireless warrior for the happiness of our country, for the freedom and happiness of the proletarians of all lands.

Women are an unrivalled force, and it would be a good thing if thousands of women followed your example.

Good wishes.

1935

OUTSTANDING DATES IN GORKY'S LIFE

1868   Born March 28, Alexei Maximovich Peshkov, in Nizhni Novgorod, on the Volga.

1872   Death of his father, a paperhanger.

1878   Death of his mother. Works as an errand-boy in a shoe store.

1880   Works as a cook's helper on a Volga steamer; the cook encourages him to read.

1881-1882   Works as a bird-catcher, a clerk in a library, an ikon painter's apprentice.

1884   Penniless, in Kazan, he lives with itinerant workers and outcasts on the embankment. In the autumn he works as a baker's helper.

1888   Becoming acquainted with a number of revolutionists, he tries to spread propaganda among the peasants. Resumes his wandering. Works as a fisherman on the shores of the Caspian Sea.

1888-1889   Becomes a night watchman in a railway yard, and a checkweighman.

1889   Arrested and detained at the prison of Nizhni Novgorod. Travels on the Volga, the Don region, the Crimea and the Caucasus.

1890   Becomes acquainted with the writer Korolenko.

1892   The Tiflis paper *Kavkaz* publishes his first story, *Makar Chudra*. Adopts pen name, Maxim Gorky (Maxim the Bitter One).

Culture and the People

1893-1894 Writes a number of stories including *Grandfather Arkip and Lenka, My Travelling Companion.*

1895 *Chelkash.*

The Song of the Falcon.

Old Izergill.

On a Raft.

1895-1896 Writes many feuilletons and stories for journals in Samara, Odessa, etc.

1896 Stricken with pulmonary tuberculosis, he goes to the Crimea for treatment.

Konovalov, etc.

1897 *Creatures That Once Were Men.*

Malva, etc.

1898 First collection of stories published in two volumes. Begins correspondence with Andreyev. Imprisoned in Tiflis for revolutionary activity; released, but under police surveillance.

1899 Meets Chekhov.

Twenty Six Men and a Girl.

Foma Gordeyev.

1900 Meets Tolstoy in Moscow.

Three of Them.

1901 *Song of the Stormy Petrel.*

Jailed on charge of issuing mimeographed leaflet addressed to the workers of Sormovo.

1902 Exiled to Arzamas. Elected to the Academy of Sciences, his election is annulled by the Tsar. Establishes contact with Russian Social-Democratic Party.

Smug Citizens, produced in Russia and abroad.

Lower Depths.

Outstanding Dates

1903-1904   Many editions of his works.

Appearance of first volume issued by *Znanie* (Knowledge), publishing house founded by Gorky.

Man.

1905   *Notes on Philistinism.*

Jailed in Peter and Paul Fortress in St. Petersburg for having written a proclamation against the government two days after Bloody Sunday (Jan. 22), but international protest forces his release.

Children of the Sun, written in prison.

Becomes one of organisers of Bolshevik daily paper, *New Life,* under Lenin's direction. Takes part in December uprising in Moscow.

1906   After collapse of revolution, he is forced to go abroad. Makes a tour of the United States to collect funds for the Bolshevik Party. In October he goes to island of Capri, in Italy, because of ill-health.

Enemies.

The Russian Tsar.

Comrade!

The City of the Yellow Devil.

La Belle France.

A political exile.

1907   Participates in London Congress of Russian Social-Democratic Party. Draws closer to Lenin. Beginning of correspondence with Lenin.

Mother.

The Ninth (Twenty-Second) of January.

1908   Visited by Lenin at Capri.

Attracted to "god-seeking," reflected in his novel, *The*

Confession, but later rejects such ideas.
Soldiers.

1909 *The Life of a Superfluous Man.*
1910 *Vassa Zheleznova.*
1911 Publishes a volume of stories.
The Life of Matvey Kozhemyakin.
Works on Bolshevik periodical, *Zvezda* (Star).
1913 Due to political amnesty, he is permitted to return to Russia, arriving December 31. Literary editor of Bolshevik review, *Enlightenment.*
Across Russia.
About "Karamazovism."
Patron.
1914 *My Childhood* completed.
Writes preface to the first collection of proletarian writers.
1915 Editor-in-chief of first internationalist review, *Annals,* in war period.
1916 *Earning My Bread,* etc.
1917 Founds at Petrograd the society, Culture and Liberty, "a free association for the development and diffusion of the positive sciences."
Strasti-Mordasti (Horrible, Terrible).
1917-1918 Does not immediately side with the Soviet power, but later becomes a leading supporter.
1919 Presides at a commission for improving scientists' living conditions. Head of *World Literature* series. Directs publication of the library of works, *Life of the World.*
Reminiscences of Leo Tolstoy.
1921 Due to recurrence of his old ailment, he goes abroad, at Lenin's insistence.

Outstanding Dates

1922 *Leonid Andreyev.*
      V. G. Korolenko.

1923 *My Universities.*

1924 Publishes a number of pieces including *V. I. Lenin.**
      Goes to Sorrento, Italy.

1925 *Rise and Fall of Artamonovs* (in English translation
      entitled *Decadence*).

1926 *L. B. Krassin.*

1927 *The Life of Clim Samghin,* Book I (*The Bystander*).
      Begins his series of publicist articles in defence of the
      Soviet Union.**

1928 *Samghin,* Book II (*The Magnet*).
      Returns to U.S.S.R. on his 60th birthday.

1929 Chosen member of the Central Executive Committee
      at the Fifth Congress of the Soviets of the U.S.S.R.
      Helps many Soviet writers.

1930 Founds review, *Abroad.* Library of Novels issued under
      his direction.
      Samghin, Book III (*Other Fires*).

1931 Decision of Central Committee of the Communist Party
      of the Soviet Union to publish *History of the Civil War
      in the U.S.S.R.,* under Gorky's initiative.

1932 *Yegor Bulichoff.****
      Fortieth anniversary of his literary career celebrated
      throughout the republics: renaming of his birthplace
      and main street in Moscow, Gorky; founding of literary
      institute, scholarships for the study of literature, etc.

---

* See *Days With Lenin* by Maxim Gorky (N.Y. and London, 1932).
** Many of them are contained in the present volume and in *On Guard for
the Soviet Union* (N.Y. and London, 1933).
*** In *The Last Plays of Maxim Gorky* (N.Y. and London, 1937).

Culture and the People

1933 *Dostigaeff and the Others.**
1934 Gorky guides the work of the First Congress of Soviet Writers.
Soviet Literature.
1936 Death June 18 in Moscow. Mourned by government and peoples of U.S.S.R.
Samghin, Book IV (*The Spectre*).
1938 At treason trial, evidence is disclosed proving that his health was undermined and his death hastened by physicians and his secretary,** as part of the plot to kill leading Soviet figures.

* *Ibid.*
** Their confessions may be read in *Traitors on Trial: Report of the Proceedings of the Case of the Anti-Soviet Bloc of Rights and Trotskyites,* pp. 525 et. seq., 584-588.